The Exemplary Teacher

Joy Based Skill Improvement for all Learning Environments

David E. McNamara, MD

Neason Hill Press

The Exemplary Teacher

First Paperback Edition

An Imprint of the Neason Hill Press

A Division of DMI

Library of Congress Cataloging-in-Publication Data has been applied for.

ISBN: 978-0-9826982-0-4

10 9 8 7 6 5 4 3

DEM

Introduction to the Exemplary Teacher

"A teacher affects eternity: she never knows where her influence stops." Henry Brooks Adams

The core attributes of all exemplary teachers are the same. They are not dependent on the subject, the learners, or the setting. An analysis of all outstanding teachers reveals many similarities despite the variables mentioned above. Teaching excellence is achievable for all who are willing to work on improving the core components and for those who find joy in the effort. In step-by-step detail we will go over the core competencies of teaching excellence, along with exercises to improve proficiency. My goal is for every reader of this book is threefold: first; a dramatic improvement in one's ability as a teacher, second; a marked improvement in one's confidence in all teaching sessions, and third; an increase in the joy derived from successfully imparting new knowledge and skill to the learner.

We learn on three levels. First there is "Informational Learning". That is, you attend a lecture on the parts of a boat and, if you master the material, on evaluation you are able to recall boat anatomy. The test might have a picture of a boat with arrows drawn to blank lines that need to be filled in by the learner. Nearly all of our formal education from kindergarten to graduate school and beyond is on this level.

The second level of learning is "Conceptual Learning". This is where we learn the principles that govern why a boat floats in water. If you master the concept of why certain objects float while others may not you might anticipate a test where you are given known or new objects and asked to predict whether they will float. "Conceptual Learning" is more difficult for most people but it is easily mastered with the proper guidance and reinforcement, and it offers unlimited joy and possibilities to the student.

On the third level there is what I call "Transformational Learning". This, by far, is my favorite. "Transformational Learning" is extremely fun because it changes how the learner behaves as its key outcome. As an example of Transformational Learning let's assume for a moment that you are teaching surgeons how to do appendectomies. Traditionally this is done by incision that leaves a scar, has a longer recovery, and some other drawbacks. Then the teacher comes to the operating room with a fiber optic scope that allows the procedure to be done through a much smaller incision, and when done properly in the correct circumstances, offers better outcomes. After the surgeon-students take your course they are "transformed" in how they approach abdominal surgery. Hopefully you will be "transformed" in how you teach your students after you read this book. Your transformation is the goal of this book!

We are all teachers on some level. For many of us we devote our livelihood to teaching others. For others, teaching is part of what we do. And for many of us teaching is not a formal part of our employment, but rather what we do with our kids, our associates, and others. As we all know teaching gets variable recognition in our society at best. There is nothing more important in my opinion than to transform a student's life through learning. Nevertheless most would agree that society has not reached the same consensus when it comes to the profession of teaching. In many settings teachers tend to be under-appreciated, overworked, and underpaid. And although recognition and compensation are important and need to be improved I would believe that the best teachers chose to teach for other reasons. After all, where would any of us be today if not for our teachers?

There is one additional point I would like to make in this introduction. Please consider the ideas and concepts presented in this book like you would a shoe. Not everything here will work for you. Hopefully some of the ideas presented will be helpful. Please take the ideas, concepts, lessons, and suggestions here and use the ones that work for you ignoring the ones that don't. As the old saying goes- "if the shoe fits ". I only ask your indulgence in giving each new "shoe" its fair chance.

Now, with excitement to begin I end this introduction and hope you will join me in mastering the material, which follows.

David E. McNamara, MD

Chapter One

A Love of the Game

"We cannot hold a torch to light another's path without brightening our own." Ben Sweetland

Some time ago in a town near to where I lived a youth golf program was offered. Kids under twelve years of age could sign up for a small fee and then for two evenings a week for part of the summer they were given golf instruction. The program was sponsored by the Parks Department and was one piece of an overall summer recreation program. The teacher of the golf program was a gym teacher from the local school system who was willing to baby-sit some kids that didn't get into one of the more popular programs. His primary reason for taking the summer job was to put a little extra money into his pocket.

Each year about 10 kids signed up for the program and by the end of the summer 4 or 5 remained. Please remember that at the time that this program was offered golf was not as popular as it is today. Additionally, the gym teacher didn't really like golf, thought of it more as a game than a "true" sport, and viewed the kids that signed up as kids that couldn't make it in Little League baseball or youth soccer, which were also offered during the summer.

The format of the teacher's instruction was to gather the kids in a circle and lecture them about the mechanics of the golf swing. He demonstrated at length the grip, the stance, and the various positions of the head, shoulders, and body during the swing. Over and over he told the kids that golf was a difficult game to master. Then, for about ten minutes at the end of the hour, the kids toiled on the driving range trying to hit the ball with their drivers and irons. The gym teacher went from student to student trying to correct each youth's many swing mistakes. It seemed hopeless and frankly it was. At the end of the session kids ran to waiting station wagons to be whisked away. Maybe you recall being a student in a program like this in some subject, golf or otherwise, at some time in your life. Maybe you remember how it felt. Nevertheless, after about three summers in this community the golf program was discontinued due to lack of interest. Youth soccer was becoming increasingly popular and the gym teacher decided he would make his money coaching a youth soccer team.

At about the same time one of the local residents whose children had been excellent students and athletes expressed an interest in teaching golf to community youths in a summer program. Since her own kids were college age she was looking for a new project to take on during the summer. She approached the Park and Recreation department with her proposal. Initially they were reluctant to consider it, but when she indicated that she was offering to volunteer her time and effort, and it wouldn't cost the town anything they reluctantly agreed to let her give it a try. Given the prior experience with the earlier program no one expected much from this new one.

The new teacher absolutely loved golf. She played it with her husband, and her children whenever she could get them onto the local public course. When they traveled they incorporated golf into their activities and she credited the game with giving her the opportunity to make lifelong friends. Her daughter was an accomplished golfer and although they didn't offer a women's golf program at her college she had entered and scored well in a number of local tournaments. That being said, and despite her enthusiasm, initially the program didn't have many takers.

That first summer about eight kids signed up for the twice-weekly program. The teacher was not discouraged, however. She was delighted to have anyone to work with. Rather than lecture or demonstrate her teaching philosophy was experiential. Her thinking appeared to be: if you experience golf and you master some small skills you will love the game like I do and want to improve. So rather than lead her students to the driving range she led them to the putting green. She told them they could pick any putter they wanted from the bin. She brought golf balls in many colors and let her students pick any color they wanted and said nothing about grip or stance or technique. The only thing she said is go to the putting green and have fun. Then she said that the goal of the day was to place the ball down anywhere on the green and try to putt it into the hole using two strokes or less. She said that she would help anyone who asked and that she wanted each student to come get her when they were ready to show off their skill.

Immediately the kids broke off into a frenzy of putter choices, some long and some short, some with mallets and some with blades. Additionally, they hurried to claim their signature color ball, some of which were red and white range balls, yellow and black range balls, red balls, orange balls, and even a pink ball. After some time an interesting dynamic began. Some kids worked independently experimenting with different clubs, stances, and approaches. Some came to the teacher for guidance and it was gladly given in small bites along with words of encouragement and praise. As proficiency improved around the green a few of the students asked the teacher if they could take “the test”. What she did next was interesting. When Johnny was ready to take the test she had all the other students stand around the green and watch him and they were instructed that when his ball fell into the hole they were to cheer loudly. Then she placed his golf ball on the green and let him putt until he holed out to the cheering of the group. In short order all the others followed.

As I remember the focus on putting lasted two sessions by which time everyone had some proficiency and some were doing excellent. Next she moved everyone off the green to a distance of between five and twenty feet and taught chipping much in the same way. The kids learned some basic skills and then were allowed to experiment. At the end of the session the exercise was the same- put a ball down fifteen feet off the green and chip it onto the green, then walk up and putt until the ball is in the hole, followed by the cheering of the other students and the praise of the teacher.

This teaching method continued through the summer until the kids moved further and further away from the target and worked their way closer with praise and encouragement. And the results were spectacular. By the end of the summer a few of the boys and girls had recorded scores of "par" on some actual golf holes. Parents were asking for private lessons from the teacher. And even now many years later many of that first class of golfers still enjoy the game and play it well. In the second year fifty-nine kids signed up for summer golf and in the third year three hundred and four tried to register. I remember it well because I was in the second year of students and still enjoy golf to this day.

The question for us to consider is how can one group of students be so discouraged while another similar group do so well given very similar circumstances? After all, the group that was lead by the gym teacher used the same facilities as the group used by the mother. The time spent in learning was essentially the same. The age of the kids and their prior abilities were essentially the same from year to year. It seems obvious that most likely the differences were in the approach and techniques of the teacher and her teaching methods.

This story is interesting in that I have used it as a case study when I am meeting with teachers who are working to improve their skills. Quickly in a group we generate a list of why the gym teacher failed and the mother succeeded. What are your thoughts on this case? Picture me frantically writing your answers on the dry erase board. We will go over them in detail in the next chapters. Ready?

Chapter Two

The Beginner's Mind

"If a child is to keep alive her inborn sense of wonder, she needs the companionship of at least one adult who can share it, rediscovering with her the joy, the excitement, and the mystery of the world we live in." Rachel Carson

You don't have to own a Monet to appreciate the French Impressionism style of painting. Most of us can't afford these painting but we still admire them. In the same way you don't have to be a practicing Buddhist to admire the wisdom of Shunryu Suzuki. Shunryu Suzuki is one of the greatest teachers of Buddhist practice and everyone can learn from him. Among the great lessons that he taught is the concept of the "beginner's mind". He suggests that we approach all problems with a beginner's mind whether we are the teacher or the student. This allows us to take in new ideas or concepts. This encourages us to be open to new ways of looking at things no matter how knowledgeable we are about them already.

The beginner's mind can be illustrated with a parable from Buddhist teaching. A highly regarded University professor who was a knowledgeable expert on Buddhism went to visit a famous Zen master. While the master quietly served tea the expert professor talked about Zen. He discussed what he knew, what his research had shown, and what he was teaching his students. The Zen master filled the professor's teacup to the brim, and then kept pouring. The professor watched the overflowing cup until he could no longer restrain himself.

"It's over-full! No more will go in! You must stop! It is spilling out on the table!" the professor blurted.

"You are like this cup." The Zen Master replied. "How can I show you Zen unless you first empty your cup?"

And like the professor many of us walk around each day with our imaginary cup full and therefore are not open to new ideas, concepts, or thoughts. What the Zen Master tries to teach us is that by being open to new ideas or new or different ways of doing things we can be delighted by what we can accomplish. It is certainly something to think about. In teaching and learning there are traditional ways of practice. What I hope to suggest is that if our cups are empty and we approach our unique challenges with a beginner's mind then new and possibly better ideas will come to us that might be small and positive. And wouldn't that be wonderful?

Shunryu Suzuki, the great teacher, said it as follows: "In the beginner's mind there are many possibilities, but in the expert's mind there are few." So regardless of your current level of expertise in teaching it is always refreshing to consider once again your cup less than full and your mind as a beginner's mind. Then you will experience the richness of all the possible ways to grow and maybe you will even learn something that the experts didn't consider. I hope so.

The exemplary teacher approaches challenges with a beginner's mind. She thinks of her cup as empty and seeks to fill it with a new understanding.

Chapter Three

A Million Reasons to Say No

"She who dares to teach must never cease to learn." John Cotton Dana

When I meet with educators to discuss approaches to working with learners I try to draw on best practices from many settings. I ask the question of why an elementary school teacher cannot use the successful teaching methods of the Harvard Business School? I ask why a team of medical students cannot define and execute a rapid cycle quality improvement project and publish the results? I ask why an inner city classroom can't use a problem-based approach to learning United States History? I ask a field hockey coach if a learner-centric model would work for her? And I ask if a college professor can change his lecture from didactic to participatory?

Over the years many enthusiastic teachers have jumped at the chance to implement new ways of inspiring and teaching learners and I have listed a few above. But also there are teachers out there for a number of reasons, a million to be exact, that think that no new method could work for them. They are the teachers that have special students, or limited resources, or required elements, or "you name it". In other words "while it may work beautifully for others it couldn't work for me". I will be the first to agree that not all strategies for improving teaching performance and outcomes will work in all settings. But I also believe that there is no setting that I know of where practices are so ideal that there is no room for improvement. In other words if the teacher is open to ideas that may improve performance and outcomes then it simply becomes the old shoe store sales pitch: view the ideas here as a shoes for you to try- if it fits for you then wear it.

One of my professors in medical school told our first year class that half of everything he would teach us would later prove to be wrong and the problem was at that time he didn't know which half it would be. That is the nature of an evolving field that is in the constant process of discovery and I admired him for admitting it. Education is an evolving field that is also in the process of discovery but I hope that more than half of the ideas in this book will prove useful for you. With the wisdom of the shoe salesman hopefully you will have a lot of new shoes to try.

But rejecting an idea without due consideration is not a helpful process. My question is not for you to tell me why this or that idea might not work in your setting? That is just too easy. Anyone can think of a million reasons why something might not work in any given scenario. My question is for you to tell me how this or that idea might be incorporated into your unique situation? When you answer this question then you reveal your true genius.

Former President Ronald Reagan proposed a number of initiatives when he was our nation's leader and many of them were met with a million reasons why they couldn't be implemented or wouldn't work if they were. He was fond of responding with a familiar quote: "Any jackass can kick down a barn. It takes a carpenter to build one up." In barn building and improving our teaching skills we want to try to always think more like "carpenters" and less like the alternative. In this way we will always be adding value to the situation rather than listing reasons that progress cannot be made.

Exemplary teachers make improvements in processes, skills, methods, and outcomes despite the many obstacles that they face. They think in terms of how they can accomplish something rather than listing reasons for why they are unable to succeed.

Chapter Four

Four Legs of a Stool: Deconstructing the Idealized in Form and Process

"Anyone who stops learning is old, whether at twenty or eighty. Anyone who keeps learning stays young." Henry Ford

I have always found that teaching to an "ideal" that is agreed upon in advance by the entire class allows for the best results. For example, with regards to the golf instructor of a prior chapter, one might ask: what are the attributes of an outstanding golf instructor? Then, with someone at the dry-erase board, students could volunteer what is important for them. I might say "patience", and you might say "love of the game", and the person next to you might say "an excellent player", and the next person "certification as a teacher" and so forth. What you might also find, as I have many times when I have approached subjects in this way, is that even the most diverse groups of learners often come up with very similar answers. When you incorporate this into the things you teach I expect you will find the same.

Deconstructing the ideal can be helpful for a number of reasons. First it reveals for the teacher the expectations of the learners. Second, it causes “buy in” from the students. After all, a student would say, I told you what I was hoping for in a golf instructor, and since you tried to live up to my expectations, I am going to try harder to succeed in your lessons. And third, it puts the teacher and the students on the same path and aligns them in terms of expectations.

When I used to teach medical students and residents I always liked to start each new class off by deconstructing the ideal patient and the ideal physician. The students loved to brainstorm at the board on both subjects and often their answers produced laughter for what it revealed about the way that some of the learners felt. But in the end the descriptive words about the ideal patient and the ideal doctor were remarkably consistent from year to year and from class to class.

In the same way let's think first about the ideal teacher from the perspective of the student and then the ideal student from the perspective of the teacher. Take a minute and write ten or fifteen attributes for each on a blank piece of paper. When you have completed this small exercise reflect on your answers and think about whether it was helpful to think in this way.

If you are like most people and you answered seriously your answers are likely to include attributes that fall into four main categories. Look at your list of words describing an "ideal teacher" and see if any fit into under the following headings. The first heading would be knowledge or mastery of the material. I call this "Knowledge Base". Typical words that might fall in this heading are: "bright", "knows the subject", "experienced", "a good resource", etc. You probably can think of better terms than those but "Knowledge Base" is a key attribute of all good teachers. After all, we don't want to take French lessons from someone who can't speak or understand French.

The next major heading that most people's descriptive words fit is "Skill Set". All great teachers have developed "skills" in helping the student master the subject. I distinguish "skill set" from "knowledge base" in the following way. Consider a neurosurgeon; of course we expect her to have knowledge of the conditions and diseases that she must treat but surgical skill is a completely different attribute separate from knowledge. I wouldn't want the most knowledgeable neurosurgeon in the world operating on me if her hand shakes when she holds the scalpel. In the same way you may know every Supreme Court case in history but if you cannot organize an effective lesson plan you cannot be an outstanding constitutional law professor. Words that typically relate to "skill set" include "effective", "organized", "able to identify students with problems" etc. Again, your examples are probably better than mine. Suffice it to say the brightest teacher in the world needs certain "skill sets" to be outstanding. These skill sets often are specific to the teaching challenge, e.g. teaching inner city middle school, vs., teaching surgery residents, vs. teaching childbirth classes. But in every situation once the skill set needed is identified and pursued the rewards often can be large.

The next major heading that the brainstorming words usually fall under is "Communication". In all professions, and especially teaching, proficiency in communication is critical for success. By communication I mean to suggest an expanded definition that includes effective and empathic listening, and the ability through clear example and analogy to make a concept or idea very real and understandable for the learner. The words usually listed here include; "good listener", "teaches in a way that I understand", and others. I hope that you get my drift here. We all can improve our listening and communication abilities regardless of what we teach.

And the final heading that your words may fall under is a category I like to call "Citizenship". In other words is the ideal teacher someone who is a part of the bigger learning community? If they teach political science do they participate in student forums that include political discourse? If they teach at a veterinary school do they volunteer at the local animal shelter? Additionally, are they engaged in a process of continuous lifelong learning or positive self-improvement? Is the community better off because they teach there, or do they drive in from the suburb, park in the locked garage, give their lecture, and leave? This is a key attribute that over and over again students identify with outstanding teachers. Additionally, in this category I would include "Good Path" attributes that I will cover in detail later but these include respect of the teacher-student relationship, boundary issues, and codes of conduct. Teachers are granted special privileges by society, and those privileges are granted based on a sacred trust. The student is almost always the vulnerable party in the relationship and all outstanding teachers recognize this and understand it as a part of her "citizenship" obligations. Words that brainstormers use to describe citizenship include "care", "involved", "leadership", and "trustworthy". Again, you may have your own word choices here and that is perfect.

So, in conclusion, by this method have we deconstructed the "ideal teacher". Think of this exercise as creating four legs of a stool. The first leg is "knowledge base". Put whatever words here that make sense for your ideal. The second leg is "skill set", and as we have already learned, this may be specific to whatever environment your ideal teacher faces. The third is "communication aptitude" and this is self explanatory, however often a difficult ability to master. And the fourth is "citizenship", a critical and important characteristic of all outstanding teachers. So, in my "good, better, best scenario" if your ideal teacher's symbolic stool has one leg she is "good", two legs "better", three legs "best", and four legs "ideal or exemplary".

"Exemplary" is an achievable goal for those who wish to strive for it. The words that you and your students use to define each of the categories are unique but helpful in understanding its composition. Knowing the components by deconstruction is the first step on the path to obtaining it. If the idea of deconstruction of the ideal is helpful to you I hope you will use it in other goal setting challenges.

Exemplary teachers excel at "all four legs" of the idealized imaginary stool. These legs include (1) Knowledge-base, (2) Skill set, (3) Communication Abilities, and (4) Citizenship.

Chapter Five

Nine Myths Revealed

"The important thing is not so much that every pupil should be taught, as that every pupil should be given the wish to learn."
John Lubbock

When I was in high school there was a student in my class that received a perfect score on his SATs. He was a student that could master almost any subject immediately. He had a near photographic memory. He was accepted at all the Ivy League Colleges and he sailed through his undergraduate course of study at Harvard. Then as a graduate student he was asked to teach a number of courses in his area of specialty. That is when things began to crumble. He couldn't understand how bright undergraduates had so much trouble with simple concepts. He couldn't accept that his students were not able to read thousands of pages in a weekend like he easily could. He struggled to explain things that were self-evident to him. The reviews that his students gave at the end of the semester were not favorable. This story has a good ending, however. With some help and a good mentor he learned how to prepare his lessons, how to teach the material to the needs and abilities of his students, and how to assist those who needed help. He worked hard at improving and continued to struggle initially but later succeeded. Actually he did so well that he went on to become a full-time teacher at a prestigious college. And the many awards that he subsequently received for teaching excellence did not derive from his native intelligence, rather from his drive and desire to master his teaching and communication skills.

Despite the good ending to this story it illustrates the first myth of the exemplary teacher: *The best students make the best teachers*. As we learned in the last chapter teaching is not only knowledge, or quickness of mind. That is only one leg of the proverbial stool, and it may help, but it is insufficient. I have seen this over and over again in consulting work that I have done to improve the teaching of medical students and doctors. The presumption, like in many industries, is that any smart person can lead students to mastery, and that "teaching" is not a specialized skill. It simply is not true. Exemplary teaching must be mastered, and extremely bright people sometimes have a harder time teaching others than those of ordinary intelligence. So now you are equipped with the ultimate excuse: if you have any setbacks on your path to being an exemplary teacher it must be because you are so extremely bright and that makes it more difficult for you!

Another myth that is a natural offshoot of the first one is *The Most Talented People make the Best Teachers.* We seem to learn this over and over again when we watch star athletes retire and become coaches. I once had a music teacher with who had perfect pitch. She was always frustrated with me when I couldn't maintain even a simple tune. People who are extremely talented, and especially if their gift seems to arise naturally, sometimes struggle to teach others to do the same things that they do. This is not to say that extremely bright and extremely talented people can't be exemplary teachers.

They can. But it is a myth that it will happen automatically. It usually doesn't.

The third myth of the exemplary teachers is that *For Some Individuals Outstanding Teaching Comes Easy*. This is the myth of the natural teacher. It arises from the fact that when we witness teaching excellence it appears to flow so easily or naturally. We've all had professors who mesmerize us with their teaching talent seeming to make difficult or complex ideas simple and allowing us to master things we didn't think possible. I can tell you that over the last few years I have worked with outstanding teachers from public schools, from sports and coaching, from Colleges and Universities, and from graduate, law and medical schools and there is unanimous agreement on this point; teaching excellence involves hard work, preparation, understanding the needs of the learners, and constant and dedicated self reflection and improvement. Teachers who appear to teach with ease get there because they have worked hard to master their specialty.

The next myth, although subconsciously believed by many, seems ridiculous when looked at carefully. It is that

Once a Certain Level of Competence is Achieved No Further Improvement is Needed. This idea could also be known as the "good enough" myth and it manifests as follows. When the curriculum is straightforward, or mandatory, or prescribed by someone else, the only thing the teacher can do is be a "conduit" over which the material is given to the learners. This is a common refrain that I often hear from teachers that are mandated to teach a certain curriculum. It couldn't be further from the truth. Exemplary teachers can "add value" no matter what the circumstances. Actually the adding of value to existing material is a core attribute of the most gifted teachers.

Next consider the myth: *Teaching is not for Shy or Introverted People.* Like the other myths this one is refuted by the many outstanding teachers who are quiet, reserved, shy, or introverted and everyday stand before large or difficult audiences and engage them thoroughly. In later chapters we will talk about ways that even shy people can succeed in front of all kinds of learners.

A common myth that needs rethinking is one that is commonly stated by frustrated educators: *Some students just can't learn*. This myth, while being untrue, is destructive because it blames the learner for suboptimal outcomes. It is a fact that some students are not interested in the subject or goals, some are disruptive and should be separated from the class, and many students learn at different rates and in different ways. Nevertheless, all exemplary teachers believe that every student is capable of learning. Everyday when students show up at the "learning meadow" they bring with them all of their problems, beliefs, doubts, and fears that are a part of their larger life. Often these issues are serious impediments to learning and are beyond the scope of that day's teacher. It doesn't mean that they can't learn, however. Exemplary teachers understand this and they relish the challenge of engaging and guiding them on a path to mastery. It has been said by the Chinese philosopher Lao-tzu "A journey of many miles begins with a single step".

Another myth that is out there is that *Exemplary and Outstanding Teachers are recognized and rewarded.* This may be the view of the general public but it is far from the truth. It is true that exemplary and outstanding teachers should be recognized, honored, rewarded financially and otherwise, but the truth of the matter is that most simply toil unnoticed. Also, in many teaching environments, systems are in place that don't allow for the best to be distinguished from the ordinary. Many outstanding teachers when they are recognized will tell you that they do not expect any special treatment or reward. I know of no instance when sincere accolades are not appreciated and accepted. I would love to see an environment where exemplary and outstanding teachers receive meaningful recognition for their contributions.

The next myth I want to discuss seems to be loosing steam on its own but used to be stated fairly frequently. That is, *Teaching is a Dead End Job*. When I was in college the brightest people became doctors, or maybe lawyers. In subsequent generations the brightest students were attracted to business and finance or maybe computer science. In my day teaching was not considered a first choice for a career. I can specifically remember when a friend of mine, who could have attended any law school or medical school decided that she wanted to be a teacher. At the time she received a lot of criticism for her choice but over the years she has been extremely successful and has made a tremendous difference for thousands of learners. When she gives talks to those considering teaching as a career she emphasizes how wise a choice it was for her and how personally rewarding it has been. After all any career is what you make of it and that leads to the last myth I would like to cover.

Teaching can be done without passion. If there is any myth out there that needs to be dispelled this may be the most important. In addition to communicating subject material, and a process for mastery, a love of the topic is a key ingredient to teaching success. I have seen over and over that passion is contagious when it comes to teaching excellence. If you have it your learners will catch it. Passion can manifest in different ways and the form it takes does not have to be flowery or over the top. It can be subtle or obvious and it is unique to the teacher. It is my experience, however, that all exemplary teachers have it.

Chapter Six

It's Not What You Might Expect

"Give me a lever long enough and a place to stand and I will move the entire earth." Archimedes

Some time ago I spent an afternoon at a famous coffee shop picking the brains of a group of outstanding teachers from troubled schools in the inner city. One was an elementary school teacher from one of the toughest neighborhoods in Baltimore. One was a middle school teacher from Detroit, and three of the others were high school teachers from Washington, DC. The conference that we were attending was in Cleveland and it was a snowy day.

Each of the teachers that I spoke with on that day had been recognized as the most outstanding in their respective schools. And a number of them were presenting at the conference that I spoke of above. The thing that struck me as the most surprising about that day was how positive they all were. Don't get me wrong they were not delusional. Each would gladly go over the myriad problems that they faced everyday in their respective schools. One of the teachers reported having been shot in the leg by a student. Another said that she constantly needed to buy simple school materials including books, paper, and pens for her classroom, despite the highest per pupil school expenditures in the nation. The third reported that at her school students were more likely to go to jail or become pregnant than finish high school.

I was able to confirm these claims relatively easily. It turns out that many public school teachers buy supplies for their students, despite the fact that per pupil expenditures are high. It turns out that a large chunk of the money goes to expenditures that don't directly benefit the typical student so glaring deficiencies defying common sense are often found when operational allocations are reviewed. Also, in the inner cities of our great country the teen pregnancy rate, violent crime, and school drop out rates are troubling to anyone who believes education is the path to a better life. Nevertheless, these issues represent the tip of the symbolic iceberg when it comes to barriers to learning according to these outstanding teachers. Students who come from suboptimal homes, or where parents are distressed or absent have difficulty in school. Students who live in a world that is violent or without positive role models may struggle to learn. Fear, hunger, and fatigue are stronger instincts than focus and a student who can't minimally focus is not a student who can progress. In addition students who do not have a core belief in education as a way to a better life are not aligned with the learning process.

As a result anyone who is willing to spend time learning about the problems of our inner city schools can very quickly become discouraged because these problems can be overwhelming. It appears that little progress is being made to improve things despite some high quality and some not so high quality efforts in this regard. In spite of these and other overwhelming issues that frustrate dedicated public school teachers everyday my sense from meeting with these teachers on that snowy day was twofold. First, they didn't spend much time focusing on the colossal obstacles to student success. They seemed to accept them, hoped they would improve, but were realistic about the prospects that suddenly we would wake up as a nation and reform our most troubled schools. And second, they were extremely positive. Seeing this I was shocked. It didn't make sense given the headwinds they faced daily. So, I needed to learn more.

The teacher who had been shot by a student years earlier told me about a pupil of hers that could not read when he entered the eighth grade and now he is attending college. These three teachers related stories of pupils that they have had that despite the odds have become doctors, and judges, and college professors. One told me about a physician who was a pupil of hers who came back to the class twice a year and told the class that she had turned around his life because of her. The elementary school teacher talked about when she saw students experience the "joy" of mastery for the first time.

In a world where it is very easy to conclude that the glass is nearly empty somehow these individuals had become convinced that not only was it half full, it was 99% full. It is remarkable when you think of it, because almost anyone in our society given the task that they faced daily would come to an opposite conclusion. So what was it that motivated these individuals so powerfully to mine for the most rare of pearls against such difficult odds?

When I posed this question to my friends on that snowy day the middle-aged woman with the limp wanted to answer first. She wanted to tell me the story of the starfish and as she was talking I noticed that she had a small silver colored starfish pinned to her collar. I think the others in the group had heard the story before but they listened politely.

Many years ago there were two individuals who walked a long and sandy beach on a hot summer day. The tide had risen earlier in the day to a very high level and had now receded. The midday sun was high and bright and there were no clouds to block its strength. The water was clear and the white sand stretched for a long way. The two walked in the firm sand just below the line that the high tide had left and enjoyed the salt air and the sound and the curl of the waves and the run of the water that occasionally washed their footprints. The older man periodically reached down and tossed an object into the sea and for a time his younger friend said nothing, but when he realized that the older fellow persisted he looked closer to see exactly what he was doing. The young man followed the older man above the tide line to the parched sand and watched him pick up a starfish that had been stranded above the high water line. And then with a strong grip and a fine throwing motion he tossed the creature into the sea. At this point the younger man noticed that the tide line was littered with stranded starfish for as far as his eye could see. There were literally thousands of stranded starfish. Seeing that the young man turned to older man and questioned him.

"What are you doing old man?"

At that moment the old man was tossing a starfish into the ocean.

"I am throwing a Starfish into the ocean where she belongs."

The young fellow was a logical and analytical thinker and was almost always correct. He looked down the white sand beach and saw thousands of starfish baking in the unrelenting sun. So he spoke.

"Old man, there are literally thousands of starfish on this beach, maybe tens of thousands. You cannot possibly help all of them, can you?"

The young man knew he was right so he was not surprised when the old man paused for quite a while before answering. The older man picked up another starfish and tossed it deep into the green water. He turned to his young friend as softly spoke. "Maybe so, but I just saved that one."

The old man smiled with satisfaction. The young man thought about the wisdom that he had just learned.

After the teacher who limped related this story the table was quiet. She picked up her coffee and took a sip. I feel that I had learned much from them and their story and saw how they had achieved such success despite the colossal expectations of failure. It reminded me of a great basketball coach and teacher who related that he got just as much or more joy from teaching a beginner how to shoot a lay up and celebrating that success as he did from helping a professional player improve his defensive skills to the point of being named to an all star team. After meeting the exemplary teachers from the inner city schools that day I feel I have a new understanding of what the coach meant by his statement.

Exemplary teachers are realistic about the odds against success but do not focus on them. Rather they concentrate on each individual pupil, and to the extent that they are able to make forward progress they celebrate that result with great joy. Small victories under difficult circumstances are meaningful outcomes, and in some ways more precious than large victories when all the stars are aligned. In a society that focuses all her energy on large victories the small successes of outstanding teachers are often overlooked. The exemplary teacher needs a strong internal compass that sometimes measures outcomes

in inches, not miles, and has a positive attitude throughout it all.

Chapter Seven

Revisiting the Four Legged Stool

"The teacher who is indeed wise does not bid you to enter the house of wisdom but rather leads you to the threshold of your mind." Kahlil Gibran

The last time I was fly fishing in Western Montana I went with an outstanding guide and teacher. Let's go through some of the reasons why he is an exemplary teacher. First, he grew up in the area and had been fishing the great rivers for over twenty years. He had knowledge of all of the species of trout and all of the fish's preference in diet. He knew the secret trails to the best fishing spots and he knew the geology and climatology of the area. Not only was he very knowledgeable of his subject but he also reflected joy in his understanding and loved to share it with his student. But here is an important point. He didn't preach his knowledge or disseminate it in a boastful way. Rather he was happy to share if his student wanted to learn, and if not he happily discussed other topics.

The trail that we followed on that day was narrow and infrequently traveled. It led to a steep hill that opened to a sunlit part of the stream. The two of us walked the trail to the stream. We arrived and there were no other people fishing the area. Rather than talk about fly-fishing I think we were discussing baseball. He let me lead the conversation. The river ran clear and had the slightly blue green color that resulted from the slate and sediment that formed the stream-bed. Additionally the bottom was covered with pebbles, shiny stones, larger rocks, and boulders that protruded out the surface of the water in spots. In some places the water ran fast and shallow. In other places pools formed beyond a fallen tree or a boulder and the water was relatively still and deep.

My guide crouched by the side of the stream, turned over a rock and studied what he saw below. This sparked my interest and I stood by to learn from him. He told me that the trout fed mostly below the surface and we could learn what was available by looking under these rocks. We also studied the insects landing on the water so he would know what things to imitate with his fly tying. He showed great skill in assessing the water conditions and the day's nymphs and insects and accurately reproduced them with great detail making flies as he sat on a rock. He was very happy to show me the bugs he was trying to duplicate and made certain that I was able to tie the flies also before we went to the river.

When we waded into the cool current he watched me cast. I do not fly fish everyday and I know he saw many things that I could improve. Nevertheless he said nothing. I watched him cast into one of the deep pools and almost immediately I saw a trout rise and bite his hook. He carefully removed the hook from the captured fish, remarked about its beauty, and when it had regained its bearings gently released it into the current. It was clear to me that he greatly admired and respected his surroundings and the beautiful fish with which he battled. I asked him to help me with my technique and he made a few small suggestions and before long I was catching fish. I cannot tell you how helpful it was having such a skilled guide and teacher as I did that day. When we walked back along the trail across the steep ravine and through the pine forest he praised me for my success and expressed gratitude for the time we were able to spend together. We walked along a trail that paralleled the bank of the same river a half-mile or so downstream from where we fished. It seemed to me that the fisherman that lined the bank and who had waded into the deeper water looked only marginally successful. Some looked frustrated.

I relate this story to share the four pillars of the exemplary teacher again. And hopefully I can expound on a few tidbits that bring these principles into focus. First consider “knowledge base”. My fly-fishing guide was very knowledgeable about every aspect of our trip. He knew the terrain. He knew the history of the river and its geology. He knew the fish and he respected and admired them. And importantly he was not boastful or conceited about his knowledge. He was happy to share it but didn’t assume his student wanted it shared. An important point is that solicited information is much better received than unsolicited information. Remember sometimes the learner may prefer to talk about baseball.

With regard to "skill set" my guide had skill in analyzing the river and where we were likely to find fish. He had skill in evaluating the local environment for various insects and nymphs, and he was able to skillfully and successfully reproduce these creatures when he tied his flies. He was clearly a skilled fisherman technically, and as a result of his analysis, preparation, and skill we caught a lot of fish. In all pursuits that I know results speak loudly indeed.

The third leg that supports the proverbial stool is "communication ability" and my teacher was accomplished in this area. During the course of the day he put me totally at ease. I was in a vulnerable position because of my technical deficiencies in casting but rather than make any comments about it he carefully made a few helpful suggestions. When I succeeded he praised me quietly and sincerely. When I struggled he did not focus on it. "Communication Ability" is such a critical element of teaching. My guide was a good listener and clearly communicated important information in a way that allowed me to progress and be successful. Additionally he didn't make me embarrassed or self-conscious about my deficiencies.

The last leg that supports the imaginary stool that we have related to outstanding teaching is "citizenship". On my day fly-fishing with my guide I came away with a new respect and admiration for Western Montana. I came away from the day with a new respect for the beauty of the rainbow trout and the ecosystem in which they live. The way that my guide conducted himself coupled with information that I collected on him on the Internet impressed me greatly about his commitment to preserving the wonderful ecosystem that he frequently fished.

In conclusion this guide illustrated the core attributes of all outstanding teachers and quickly won me over as someone who I would recommend to anyone fishing the rivers of Western Montana. The outstanding teacher, such as the one I have described gives much more in value than he/she takes in compensation. Remember that in my story those fishing without guides were not catching much, if anything.

Teachers like these are the ones that we admire, and attributes that this chapter illustrates are ones that we can all strive for. In this way it is possible for all of us to move from good to better to best.

The exemplary teacher always strives to improve her "knowledge base", "skill set", "communication abilities", and "citizenship". Ultimately these efforts add value to her learner's experience and result in improved outcomes.

Chapter Eight

Who are these learners, anyway?

"The only dreams impossible to reach are the ones you never pursue." Michael Deckman

We are all on a journey somewhere. We are all students in some aspects of our lives. Maybe we don't see ourselves officially in the learner category but we all are. If we don't think so we are probably in denial. Life is all about learning and adapting. Change is the only constant that we know. This lesson may be difficult for some of us to accept. But there is no alternative. For those who seek refuge from the deep waters by remaining on the shore and not venturing into the sea I have new information to share. The shore is an illusion. There is no shore. We have spent our entire lives navigating deep waters, and most of us have done so fairly well. The question for us now is what are we going to do next?

In this regard when learners arrive at your doorstep it is your job to help them find what they seek. Your doorstep may be the lecture hall or classroom. It may be a job retraining center or a research lab. It may be a church, temple, or a bus stop. Or it may literally be a doorstep. They may have arrived seeking something that others have said you possess or they may simply be assigned to your class. You may be their fist choice or their last, or they may have had no choice at all in being matched to what you have to offer.

When your learners arrive they will bring with them all of their beliefs, prejudices, doubts, and behaviors that they have acquired on their journey before they met you. They will bring their strengths, curiosity, and past successes also. If they are hungry, sleepy, poor, or abused they will bring that with them. If they have other responsibilities, commitments, or interests they will bring that with them. In short, when learners arrive they are burdened by all their prior human experience. Given the baggage that we carry with us it is remarkable that we can learn anything at all. I am particularly struck when public school teachers share the burdens that students bring with them to class everyday in America. In many schools across the USA there is not adequate peer or family support for education. Students arrive at class hungry, tired, cold, and often in fear. Teachers are expected to remediate a broken family or an abusive home situation. Try as they might it is mostly difficult and sometimes almost impossible.

Nevertheless, in every classroom, lecture hall, seminar room, or wherever learners meet teachers the teacher should be able to tell us who her learners are. She should be able to describe their strengths and weakness, and the obstacles that they face. This sometimes extends beyond the learning environment and into the home. These types of assessments help us to develop a realistic plan for each student. These assessments can be done in many ways, and whether they are formal or informal, some sort of assessment that addresses these issues should be part of every teacher's skill set.

In general and largely for reasons that we alluded to above learners fall into three main categories: "not engaged", "engaged", and "disruptive". I have found that these categories pretty much hold true whether the setting is third grade reading class or a review course for attorneys who are scheduled to take the bar exam. The teacher has three core goals: (1) Teaching to the "engaged", (2) Converting the "not engaged" to "engaged", and (3) Disposing of the "disruptive". The third is a problem that some teachers spend their entire careers working on. It is source of frustration, cynicism, and burnout for many wonderful teachers. And although solving the problem of the "disruptive" students in many settings there is neither the will nor the resources to address the issue properly.

In my experience students who are disruptive fall into two main categories. The first are the learners who master the material quickly and are bored. They disrupt other learners who are slower than they are. These learners, if they are so motivated, are often remediated when they are given extra challenges to work on. Also in counseling they sometimes have insight into their disruptive behavior and can be rewarded for making positive changes. Unfortunately, this class of "disrupters" is by far the minority. Far more common are the learners who are not the best students, who struggle, and rather than continue trying they simply make it more difficult for others. These "disrupters" have many root causes, often sad and not of their own making, however their behaviors are pernicious and ultimately can interfere with the progress of other learners. I feel strongly that disruptive students who cannot be remediated need to be removed from the learning environment. Ideally they can be rehabilitated or worked with one on one. Unfortunately teachers from all over the country tell me that when disruptive students undermine their classrooms they find themselves without answers from their supervisors and administrators. The energy drain that they can cause is so powerful that it wears on the teachers and other students. Sometimes at seminars that I have been involved in entire breakout sessions revolve around the frustration and anger that they can cause.

If our public education system is going to improve so that we are one day competitive again with other developed countries' school systems we are going to have to empower teachers so that they can focus their attention on motivated and engaged students. This means that the teacher will assess who stays and who leaves the classroom and the school administrators will back them one hundred percent. Until this happens teachers will struggle with this problem to one degree or another.

No teachers that deal with disruptive students can claim one hundred percent success but some are more effective than others. The principles of success seem to involve principles of behavioral modification. Dog trainers tell us that to stop a dog from barking it does no good to yell "No No No!" when the dog barks, but if the dog is quiet on command for a certain period of time he gets a small reward. As the dog learns to be a non-barker the quiet time to reward is lengthened. In the same way a set of rules for the "disruptive" student are established. If they are violated there is a quiet correction but not much attention. If they are followed a small reward is given with praise. In some cases the pet trainer approach can be helpful.

For a number of years I worked as a medical director for a health system. One of the joys of my job was when one of the 150 or so doctors was sent to me for complaints of disruptive behaviors. Incidentally, if you look at the underbelly of almost any profession, from policeman to paratroopers, there are a certain percentage of them that will have behavior problems on the job. Interestingly, most third grade teachers can tell you who they will be twenty years before they are in my office. When you interview these individuals often it is everyone else's fault but theirs. But it takes a lot of time and investment to train a physician or other professional so we always first try to remediate if possible. What I have found the most helpful is in a non-threatening way to get agreement on acceptable and unacceptable behaviors and expectations in writing and impose a period of careful monitoring that the physician agrees to. If the initial period of monitoring produces no further transgression then a communication of appreciation and praise is given and the monitoring period is extended. This process is repeated until the problem is unlikely to happen again. If there are further transgressions there are no emotional outbursts, rather a review of the problem and an escalation of the restrictions. In all cases the goal is to keep patients safe and well cared for while trying to be respectful of the doctor. In the same way the goal of dealing with disruptive learners should be the same, the protection of the learning environment for other students. The interventions that we take should allow the disruptive student respect and a path to redemption, and should be increased incrementally in accordance with our policies and procedures. Additionally, it is often helpful to consult school administrators and supervisors to assist in obtaining the best possible outcome for all.

The exemplary teacher strives to understand her students and is aware that they bring many challenges with them to the learning environment. Her goal is to teach to "engaged" students and bring the others around. She understands that all learning environments can have "disruptive" students and although she tries to bring them onto a better path she realizes that her ultimate goal is to create an

environment that is the most conducive for all of her students to learn.

Chapter Nine

Rethinking the "Comparison-Based" Identity

"All too often we are giving learners cut flowers when we should be teaching them to grow their own plants." John Gardner

Our entire educational system is based on the concept of a "comparison-based" identity. One might argue persuasively that our entire society is largely modeled on it also. But do we ever stop and think about the benefits and the pitfalls of such a system. If the "bell shaped" Gaussian distribution is our guiding principle and it is applied equitably then some should not pursue math while others should not pursue music. Fair enough, but is the scalpel precise enough to know where to cut? In my college days the "bell shaped curve" was followed by many of the faculty of my college like the North Star. But their results, like many of the ship captain's that followed the stars without considering the waves or the current, were less than spectacular when it came to motivating the learners.

Einstein was one of the greatest mathematicians of all time. Yet he was on the wrong side of the bell shaped curve and supposedly flunked math in school. Warren Buffet is considered the best investor of a generation yet he was turned down by his first choice for business school. Vincent Van Gogh supposedly never sold a painting in his life, unless you count the few that his brother bought from him to help him out. What would this world be like without family and friends? Study the great novelists, academy award winners, and Nobel Prize winners. They often tell a story about failure in the early subjects, poor grades, and discouragement from the system. Can we learn anything from them and apply it to how we rate learners in our roles as educators?

If our system only rewards the winners and discourages the losers based on a curve what does it predict for our society? Can educators devise a better system for evaluation that rewards success, allows for progress, and is not comparison-based? I think so. I firmly believe that our education system needs to reward the best and the brightest, and I have no doubt that it will continue to do that. But the student who goes to school cold, hungry, and afraid, and yet rises above his potential is much more interesting to me than the prep student who with every resource imaginable stumbles along below his grade level.

This is a controversial topic with more questions than answers. My goal in raising it is to continue the discussion. If we only see ourselves by how we rank against others then we are less for it. And I think educators play a big role in where this whole process goes. The story I like to tell is one of three boys who are in the room comparing their pay from their summer jobs. Each one has earned three dollars working at the lemonade stand. Each is happy because they can buy a comic book, a pack of gum, and some baseball cards. All is well with the world until a fourth boy comes in the room and announces that he was paid four dollars for a day's work. That was the beginning of the trouble for the others.

While it is foolish to deny that we all compete in the world for limited resources it often isn't that we don't have enough that is the problem, rather that someone else has more than we do. To some degree, from the time we enter a school building we are bombarded with this message. The exemplary teacher, at a minimum, is aware that the system of "comparison-based" identity is imperfect, and is thinking about new methods of evaluation that are more positive for the learners.

The exemplary teacher struggles with evaluations based on the comparison-based identity and is looking for ways to make evaluations more helpful in that they encourage students to reach, or even exceed, their potential.

Chapter Ten

Doctors and Circus Acts

"Whether you think you can, or think you can't... you are right."

Henry Ford

For some time I have really enjoyed giving seminars for practicing physicians who want to improve their teaching skills. Often as part of a larger gathering, and usually as a "break out" session I would receive a group of physicians who had signed up for my group. Over the years these breakout groups have grown quite large but the teaching principles are still the same.

In the beginning we break into two groups randomly and go to two different rooms. From each group we chose a volunteer leader and then meet briefly with each teacher. For a few minutes each group is shown a short video on how to juggle three rubber balls at once. The video shows all the steps to accomplish juggling and after it finishes it cycles continuously in the background. The same video runs in each "break out" room.

The first "teacher" is instructed to tell the audience that she has had a great deal of success in teaching doctors how to juggle and that even in a short time many participants can expect to master the task. Additionally she is introduced in a way that praises her juggling instruction credentials and teaching abilities. Remarkably, she is unable to juggle at all and has never attempted teaching juggling before. Further, she is instructed to let her students follow the video and to praise any progress that any of the doctors are able to make, no matter how slight.

The second physician "teacher" is coached to tell her class that she has no prior juggling experience, can't juggle, can't teach juggling, and that she believes that juggling is very difficult. She instructs her class to do their best and if she sees progress she is instructed to do nothing. Further she tells her class that she doesn't expect much but to have fun.

After each teacher gives her opening statement each student is given a small red, yellow, and blue rubber ball, the video is started and the rest has almost always been highly entertaining. Physicians for the most part are highly self-conscious, awkward outside their circle of competence, and generally uncoordinated. But they are also highly motivated to succeed so the combination usually makes for a barrel of laughs.

After about thirty minutes or so of mayhem we call the sessions to a close and dissect our methods and compile the results. Now I have done these sessions many times with groups large and small and the results are extremely consistent. The groups with the "qualified teacher" who speaks of success with similar students always produces more jugglers and near jugglers than the "less qualified" teacher, who often produces none. The interesting thing in these demonstrations is that the teachers are <u>not</u> different in their ability to teach juggling. The only thing that differs is the learner's perception of the teacher's ability. And, although no one suggest that any teacher mislead students on ability, it is clear in these sessions that an "expectation of success" is a powerful force.

The discussions that go on after these sessions are powerful and transformative and many of the doctors who leave these seminars have contacted me and indicated that they now always teach with an "expectation of success". So the very important conclusion is that all exemplary teachers always teach with an "expectation of success".

In a similar vein recently I interviewed an award winning third grade teacher that taught in a very poor school district. The students in her class came from the most disadvantaged circumstances imaginable. They started third grade far behind grade level by any measure. They brought with them all of the problems of inner city life. Some came from unstable homes. Some had health issues. For others English was a second language. The school where she taught was fraught with problems. The building was cold in the winter. It had broken windows. The textbooks were out of date. The information technology resources were severely lacking. Nevertheless, this particular third grade teacher managed to consistently bring her students to "grade level" and sometimes higher. When I asked her how she did it she was very clear. She always taught with an "expectation of success". She always assumed she would be able to bring her students to grade level no matter what and her belief in this regard was contagious to even third graders. She basically told her students that no matter what their situation she would work with them and that they would succeed. She knew it and made them believe it. She had done it before with students who were worse off, and she would do it again. In other words, she created a powerful "expectation of success". Needless to say that for her it wasn't rhetoric. Once she committed to her students she worked tirelessly day and night helping them overcome obstacles, deficiencies, and guiding and praising progress no matter how small. But it was an unwavering belief in the likelihood that all of her students would succeed that made her other efforts so successful.

This information is not new. It has been known as the Pygmalion or Rosenthal effect. The Pygmalion effect refers to situations in which students perform better than other students simply because they are expected to do so. The effect is named after George Bernard Shaw's play Pygmalion, in which a professor makes a bet that he can teach a poor flower girl to speak and act like an upper-class lady, and is successful.

The Pygmalion effect requires a student to internalize the expectations of their teachers. It is a form of self-fulfilling prophecy, and in this respect, students with poor expectations internalize their negative label, and those with positive labels succeed accordingly. Rosenthal conducted research as early as 1910 that showed when an elementary school teacher was told that the students were very bright it created an "expectation of success" and the students did better regardless of their prior abilities. So whether one creates student expectations for success or for failure usually they prove true.

Exemplary Teachers always create "expectations for success". They plant "seeds of belief" with their students that they can succeed.

Then they teach, teach, teach until those expectations are met.

Chapter Eleven

Fruit Trees and Storms at Sea

"If a lettuce plant does not grow, we do not blame the lettuce. Instead, the fault lies with us for not having nourished the seed properly." Buddhist proverb

A story handed down from generations before goes something as follows... In two seaside towns the communities each decide to build cathedrals. Plans are made and the money is appropriated. Each will select stone from the local quarry. Each has approximately the same budget, workforce, and architect. Each town hires a project manager, in the first town a proven builder and in the second town a retired elementary school teacher. The builder has been successful with a number of small projects in the past although nothing of this size. The teacher was the best elementary school teacher the community had ever known and is now retired.

In the beginning the building projects go well. The proven builder paces nervously and calls out mistakes as he sees them. He is determined to keep on schedule and punish those who fall behind. After all he is responsible for a big project and the communities' funds. The elementary school teacher takes a different approach. With the placement of every granite block she praises the worker and thanks him or her. When a block is placed incorrectly she guides the worker positively and when the mistake is corrected she praises and thanks the worker.

As time passed an interesting divergence occurs. The "praise and thanks" cathedral rises quickly from the ground while the "taskmaster" cathedral trails behind. As the second church starts to fall behind schedule the project manager becomes more angry and hostile to his workers. This creates resentment, further mistakes, and delays. The "praise and thanks" church sometimes experiences problems but the workers volunteer to stay late or work extra until the problem is solved. As a result this cathedral is completed ahead of schedule and under budget. The second cathedral runs into delays and cost overruns and when storms come up at sea and damaged the communities' sailing fleet attention is focused elsewhere. With funding depleted the job lays half finished and unusable.

If you are like me you prefer a completed Cathedral to one that is missing a roof, and although the story is likely fiction it illustrates an important point. Learners are like cathedrals, and they learn stone by stone like the building of a church. Praising each placement of stone results in a stronger, better built structure, that is completed sooner, and with greater joy. In this way exemplary teachers learn to praise every placement of stone no matter the size.

Think of praise as the planting of a seeds. I like to think of fruit trees. One day a small seed may grow into a large tree and bear much fruit. On the other hand criticism, which is often necessary, is like cutting the branch of a tree, or a limb, or if it is serious enough the trunk. We cannot know the value of praise and we cannot know which seed will sprout or exactly when but we should believe that the more seeds we plant and care for the more fruit will one day be harvested.

In future chapters we will explore how lesson plans can break down goals to small “bites” like the placement of individual stones in the building of a cathedral. Each student as they place a stone needs praise and encouragement. Exemplary teachers know this and teach in this way.

Exemplary teachers traffic in sincere praise, praise for progress small and large, and they never underestimate its powerful effect.

Chapter Twelve

The Magic of Social Proof

"A master can tell you what she expects of you. A teacher, though, awakens your own expectations." Patricia Neal

Anyone who has watched an infomercial on television knows about social proof. You may not have heard the name but when it is described you will recognize it. Marketing and advertising executives have marveled at the power of social proof for many years but only a small percentage of teachers know about it and fewer still have it in their teaching toolbox.

Imagine resting on your television room couch and maybe you are talking on the phone or cannot sleep. You had selected a particular program to watch but you were multitasking and the program is over. In its place is a long advertisement for a beauty product, a grilling machine, or a rotisserie oven. At first it seems ridiculous or even comical. You have no interest in such a product nor do you believe the claims they are making. But then someone fairly ordinary comes on and says the following: "I am just like you at home Mr. or Ms. Viewer. I too thought this product was ridiculous and the claims that were made were unlikely to be true but, crazy as it sounds, I took a chance and ordered the product and I was amazed that it turned out to be so wonderful."

And then another skeptical person comes on and gives a similar testimonial of how the product works for her. And then another and another and you get the message. Before the commercial is over, and largely based on the testimonials of ordinary people like ourselves, thousands of people are calling in to get their own beauty cream, acne treatment, or real estate investing course. If you take the time to watch these infomercials you can appreciate just how convincing these testimonials can be.

The use of testimonials by individuals in infomercials for marketing purposes is one form of "Social Proof". Social Proof, also known as Informational Social Influence, is a psychological phenomenon that occurs in ambiguous social situations where it is difficult for people to know how to behave. In these instances people look to surrounding people and conclude that they possess more knowledge about the situation. So they do what the surrounding people do. In the infomercial the viewer doesn't have time to evaluate the product so he defers to the people who give testimonials.

If a man is seen with many attractive women he is more likely to be rated as attractive by those who are nearby but do not know him. The observer appears to have the cognition "all those women seem to like him, so there must be something about him that is high value." Alternately, if observers see a man rejected by many women his social value or attractiveness is likely to be judged negatively by observers. Everyone remembers the scene in the movie Legally Blonde when Reese Witherspoon feigns heartbreak from a clearly unattractive male in the presence of two other women, causing the women to instantly change their behavior towards him from indifference to a high level of interest and attraction.

One particularly interesting experiment involving "Social Proof" (or the lack of it) was conducted by the

Washington Post Newspaper Staff in January of 2007. They arranged for Joshua Bell, probably the world's best living violinist and possibly musician, to put on old clothes and play violin in the D.C. metro station with his case open for tips. Normally it would cost hundreds to see Joshua Bell in concert if you could get tickets but here he played in old clothes without notoriety in an attempt to see what passer-byes would do. In other words he performed without any "social proof". The producers videotaped the entire performance and later interviewed those who stopped or tossed money into the violin case. Parenthetically, he played on a violin handcrafted by Antonio Stradivari in 1713 that was worth over 3 million dollars.

What happened was very interesting. In the three quarters of an hour that Joshua Bell played, only seven people stopped for more than a minute. Twenty-seven gave money, most of them on the run- for a total of $32 and change. Over 1000 people passed by in a rush without even turning to look. Incidentally, Joshua Bell came back to Washington, DC a few months later to accept the Avery Fisher prize, recognizing him as the best classical musician in America.

So if a virtuoso musician attracts almost no interest without social proof what does it say for the rest of us? It is critically important for us to think about how we use "social proof" to improve our ability to gain the trust and attention of our students. All exemplary teachers use the principles of "social proof" to improve their relationship with their students.

Think for a minute about a new student entering a class. She asks herself: "Who is this teacher?" "Why should I put out a large effort to learn from this teacher?" "Why should I think that participation in this class would be in my interest?" Not knowing where to find answers to these questions the prospective student looks for some level of "social proof". I visited a particularly successful 5th grade teacher who put pictures of students who where in her class and later graduated from college. These then and now pictures were very powerful "social proof" that time spent in this classroom was well spent. Especially when there were pictures of doctors, lawyers, and professors who had sat in these same small wooden chairs.

There are as many examples of "social proof" for exemplary teachers as there are exemplary teachers but they are commonly things like diplomas, pictures of prior successful students, laudatory letters from prior students, awards, framed pledges and promises, and statements from well regarded figures. The trophy cases of successful coaches like the pictures of prior newborns who made it out of the neonatal intensive care unit are powerful examples of social proof that encourages current participants to believe in the process.

Probably the most powerful example of "social proof" is the recent election of President Barrack Obama in the fall of 2008. Seeing an African American president in office sends a message to all minorities and especially African American young males that if they work hard and succeed in school then they too could be president. This version of social proof tells us that if an African American can become president then African Americans can become anything. That is an extremely powerful message.

All exemplary teachers proudly employ the force of "Social Proof" to connect with their students and help maximize their success.

Chapter Thirteen

Creating Excitement

"Nine-tenths of education is encouragement." Anatole France

Recently I had the opportunity to observe three teachers who taught American History in middle school over the course of many months. In the first two classes, a suburban and an inner city school district, both teachers did a good job of presenting the material while I was there. The third setting was rural and the teacher was unrecognized and outstanding. The subject material was early American History from before George Washington up to Abe Lincoln. All three classes had about the same number of students. The facilities were about the same, although the inner city classroom was the newest and surprisingly most up to date. It was clear to me that the inner city had the most disadvantaged students followed by the rural pupils. The suburban kids were mostly middle class. The textbooks were similar in that they were generic history books with a combination of text and pictures.

Although my visits to each classroom are only observations and are not scientific or conclusive I saw some very different approaches with different results that are worthy of sharing. It might be interesting to conduct experiments to validate what I observed but I submit to you that it probably is not necessary. After I share with you what I saw I would ask if you agree with my conclusions.

There is no doubt that each of the teachers that I observed had a good knowledge of the subject material involved. If I had to guess I would say that the suburban teacher was the most knowledgeable about early American history, but this is only based on her answering some difficult questions that the students raised. In each class there were students that were initially disengaged or disinterested, especially in the inner city. This is an area where I think the rural teacher was the most successful. In the other two settings the disengaged students were mostly ignored, learned little, and I believe earned poor grades.

In the inner city there was a student who was disruptive and interfered with the other students who wanted to learn. This was a common source of irritation and frustration for the inner city teacher who did a good job of setting limits for this student. I think that the class would have done much better if this student was removed but he was not and I don't know if this was an option that the teacher had.

In each of the classes there was a few very bright students. And at the beginning of the year there were a few very interested students in each class but as the months unfolded the rural classroom definitely had the greatest number of interested students. And this is why I share this story.

All three teachers were skilled presenters. All three teachers presented the material in chronological order and essentially followed the textbook that she had. But while the inner city and suburban teachers used almost exclusively a lecture and assigned reading approach the rural teacher used a completely different approach. First let me comment on the usual approach. I consider myself a good student and sort of a history buff but like many of the students I found myself getting board from the lectures that were intended for kids with attention spans less than mine. Nevertheless the best students hung in there and thrived, the disinterested disengaged in one way or another, and the teacher often battled with the disruptive kids.

In the rural classroom the teacher took a completely different approach. First she called her class “Fifteen Presidents” rather than “Early American History” or whatever the textbook title was. Second she asked the class to divide into two groups based on their preference to study the presidents or the first ladies in question. I would have thought that this would have fallen into two camps based on gender, but it didn’t. Then the assignment was simple. Each team would create “baseball style cards” based on the presidents or the first ladies. The pupils were told that they could put whatever they wanted on each card and it would be up to them. The teacher told me that in the early days these cards were hand made, but with increased technology, once designed they were now printed at the school resource center. The kids (and I) ate this assignment up. There were lectures, of course, and assigned readings but the goal was to come up with great presidential and first lady cards. In my group we decided to have a picture of the president, the years that he served, political affiliation, prior career, and important accomplishments. The first lady cards were similar but in some ways even more creative.

Even the kids who are normally not interested in history or even school got involved in these projects. It brought the artist, the computer person, the historian, and the athlete to the table. It taught team building skills to middle school kids. And I must say: some of these trading cards were outstanding. I would bet that kids keep their sets many years after they finish school.

So how did this outstanding teacher make middle school history such an exciting course? She told me that when she was a student she experienced boredom. She remembered teachers she had that made her classes interesting or exciting. So she constantly asked herself how she could make her material more interesting, exciting, and fun? In my view this question made all the difference in the world.

All exemplary teachers should ask the question: How can I make my subject more interesting, exciting, and fun?

Chapter Fourteen

A Ratio to Consider

"Luck favors the mind that is prepared." Louis Pasteur

No performance ever excelled without preparation. Even the simplest classroom period will fall flat if the teacher is not prepared. Learners may know less of the subject material than the teacher. They may not have the skill set that those with mastery have. They may not understand the subtleties of the material the way the teacher should. But all learners are experts in one area. They can tell if the teacher is not prepared. They can tell is the teacher is bluffing and they can tell if the teacher is winging it.

Let me give you an extreme example. I would go as far to suggest that I could take a classroom of first graders as my allies, put college professors before them to present on their usual subjects, and afterward ask them which professors were prepared and which were not. Nine times out of ten they could tell me. Not because they understood the material. Not because they understood the concepts. The reason for this is that even first graders are highly emotionally intelligent. And they can immediately spot an impostor, a faker, or someone who is not prepared.

People who are not prepared give off subtle and not so subtle cues that cannot be masked. These signals discourage learners. They send a message that the lesson is not important. It sends a message that the teacher doesn't care deeply about the learners. Preparation, practice, and rehearsal when necessary will improve and polish a performance. Students will take notice of this and appreciate it. Preparation is the friend of those armed with it. It is a very powerful ally. Lack of preparation on the other hand is the enemy of the polished performance. It is a destructive force. It may create a missed opportunity.

Although the amount of preparation necessary varies greatly from the class, the lesson plan, the subject, and other factors, I feel that a good rule of thumb is that for a one hour long class there should be about two hours of preparation. If the class is given repeatedly or from year to year the amount of preparation might be reduced. To create new material or a new lesson plan it might take three hours or more of work to create a compelling presentation. Regardless of the amount of preparation needed, anything less will immediately be discovered by the learners.

I am told that the virtuoso cellist Pablo Cassals was known to practice three hours a day even after he reached the age of ninety-two. When asked why at this late stage of his life he continued to practice so diligently he was reported to say.

"Because I think I am starting to see improvement."

In this way we should all think like Pablo Cassals and realize that practice and preparation will improve our teaching success.

The exemplary teachers always prepares before each lesson. In this way her time spent with her students is as valuable as possible.

Chapter Fifteen

The Force of a Butterfly's Wing

"One joy scatters a hundred griefs." Chinese Proverb

In education often the smallest of force can make a tremendous difference for the student if it is applied at the proper time, in the proper way, and in the proper direction. When I was a college student a well-respected professor once told me that students were like balls at the crest of a high mountain. They would all roll down the hill with the tiniest push. But, once started, they could roll down many different paths with many different outcomes. One path may lead to great success, abundance, and self-actualization. Another may lead to frustration and ruin. And in between there are paths of all possibilities.

The teacher often has the power of that initial push. The smallest action, faintly or not perceived at all, can have far reaching effects on the life and career of the student. Consider this prospect in reverse. When I interviewed many extremely successful people and asked them about their path to success I often heard a similar refrain. They hadn't started on the path that led to their success; rather a chance event occurred which put them on a "golden" route. Often that chance event led to a positive change of course in their lives and more often than not that chance event involved a teacher.

If you think this is too good to be true you are probably right. I forgot to tell you the fine print of this story. That is we don't know which one of the hundreds of small positive acts that we do as teachers will result in the student rolling down the mountain on a better trail. We can only know that sometimes it will work. And for the exemplary teacher that knowledge is enough to be constantly pushing small but positively on all students. It is a very cool equation actually even though the outcome reward is unpredictable.

The concept of small changes in initial conditions resulting in large changes in measured outcomes has a name. It is called the "Butterfly Effect". The phrase refers to the idea that a butterfly's wings might create tiny changes in the atmosphere that may ultimately alter the path of a tornado or delay, accelerate or even prevent the occurrence of a tornado in a certain location. The flapping wing represents a small change in the initial condition of the system, which causes a chain of events leading to large-scale alterations of events. Had the butterfly not flapped its wings, the trajectory of the system might have been vastly different. While the butterfly does not cause the tornado, the flap of its wings is an essential part of the initial conditions resulting in a tornado.

The term "butterfly effect" itself is related to the work of Edward Lorenz at MIT. In 1961, Lorenz was using a numerical computer model to rerun a weather prediction, when, as a shortcut on a number in the sequence, he entered the decimal .506 instead of entering the full .506127 the computer would hold. The result was a completely different weather scenario. Lorenz published his findings in a 1963 paper for the New York Academy of Sciences noting: "One meteorologist remarked that if the theory were correct, one flap of a seagull's wings could change the course of weather forever." Later speeches and papers by Lorenz used the more poetic butterfly. According to Lorenz, upon failing to provide a title for a talk he was to present at the 139th meeting of the American Association for the Advancement of Science in 1972, Philip Merilees concocted "Does the flap of a butterfly's wings in Brazil set off a tornado in Texas" as a title.

As teachers we need to remember to flap our wings in small positive ways all the time for we never know what great student outcomes can occur as a result.

The exemplary teacher is a constant wing flapper always changing the initial conditions for her learners positively. Ultimately, this results in unpredictable but dramatically beneficial outcomes for her students.

Chapter Sixteen

Purity of Path

"The essential thing is not knowledge, but character." Joseph Le Conte

The relationship between learner and teacher is a sacred one that has been held in high esteem for thousands of years. Some may say that this relationship has deteriorated lately. Others may say that teachers are not valued as highly as they should be by modern society. Both statements are true in my opinion, however an ideal relationship is a goal to be strived for and if teachers chose their professor by the likelihood of being valued by society they most likely would have veered onto another career path. Most of the outstanding teachers I have known have highly developed internal compasses and are more likely to do the right thing rather than the thing that pleases others. Unfortunately, this sometimes leads to less pay and less recognition than those receive in other callings. But in the end exemplary teachers are exemplary people who would have succeeded in any profession. They just happened to choose teaching.

By "purity of path" I am referring to a core set of values that all outstanding teachers adopt. They include full informed consent for learners, disclosure of conflicts of interest, disclosure of viewpoint, respect and adherence to all boundaries with regard to the teacher-learner relationship, adherence to a code of conduct, and the adoption and sharing of a personal and learning mission statement. In addition, I recommend that teachers have students make a pledge to the "purity of path" which addresses the ideals of student effort and conduct.

We know that all learners and teachers are human, and as such, are subject to the frailties of the human condition. But in the learning environment the relationship is between the possessor of knowledge and the vulnerable striver. It is between the grader and the vulnerable learner. It is between the person with an ideology, viewpoint, or potential conflict of interest and the uninitiated. In other words the teacher has the power and the learner is vulnerable. All exemplary teachers treasure and respect this relationship and strive to keep it pure. It is not always possible to be 100% pure because in a complex society there are a lot of grey areas, but there are many things teachers can do to keep the learning environment as pure as possible.

We have all known teachers who possess extraordinary knowledge and skill. They are outstanding communicators and may even be community leaders but when it comes to the learning environment they fail the "purity of path" equation. An example is the science professor who won't teach evolution because it conflicts with her religious beliefs. I had a political science professor that was such an ideologue that it affected how he taught his material. My colleague had a neurosurgical professor who hated poor people and would alter therapy if he knew their socio-economic status. More serious examples involve teacher's dating students and other boundary issues.

I have found that agreement in advance to the principles set forth may offer the best opportunity for teachers and learners to stay out of treacherous waters. For this reason I will describe them in detail. By informed consent I am referring to a mutually acceptable understanding of what the learner can expect from the proposed course in terms of material covered, evaluation, and expectations. The expectations can be for both the teacher and the learner and can cover such things as class attendance, timely completion of assignments, and a process for resolving a grievance should one occur.

By disclosure of conflicts of interest I mean that if a presenter is giving a keynote presentation on management of depression and is paid monies by one of the drug companies that makes a depression medicine that should always be disclosed. Conflicts of interest come up in the learning environment all the time and should not necessarily exclude teachers from the classroom. In my opinion they should always be disclosed in advance.

By disclosure of viewpoint it is important to let your students know in advance if you subscribe to a viewpoint, ideology, belief system, or a methodology that a reasonable person would want to know in advance. If you are the local president of the "flat earth society" and you teach science at the community college I believe that your "purity of path" statement should reveal your leanings. Your belief system may not interfere with your teaching but your students have a right to know so they can decide. I once had a surgery professor who didn't operate on people over the age of 85 years, but he was an otherwise good teacher, and I knew in advance that was his approach so for me there wasn't a problem. The hospital that he worked at may have evaluated him differently but that is a topic for another day.

By boundary violations I am talking about inappropriate actions that compromise the trusting relationship between student and teacher. These include teachers dating students, violating confidentiality of student records, harming students, involving students in illegal activities, and other similar items. Although the boundaries for conduct by teachers should be unambiguous we often hear of issues arising in this category. When boundaries are violated by people in society that we hope to trust the damage goes far beyond any single breach in a relationship.

I recommend that all organizations develop a "code of conduct" document that all teachers review and sign. It can be specific to the organization but should have general principles involving safe boundaries for students, and expected behaviors for teachers.

Additionally, organizations and individuals can create mission statements. This is another important way that we can make a pledge to the learner. When it comes to dental care I am a nervous patient but recently when I went to see my dentist I noticed that he had a "mission statement" on the wall in his waiting room. His mission statement revealed that many of his patients were anxious and he pledged to be gentle, caring, and understanding, among other things. It also said that he pledged to take the time necessary to answer any questions that might arise. It sounds trite but this framed document comforted me. If he took the time to put it on the wall where everyone could see it I concluded that he believed it also.

In our society teachers are given leeway in how they conduct themselves. It is not possible to oversee every moment of the teacher-learner relationship. But the reason to have a purity of path is not to avoid the penalties of its violation, rather to create the safest, most trusted relationship possible. It is in this place that learning has an opportunity to thrive.

In this way the Exemplary Teacher always strives for "Purity of Path" in her teaching environment.

Chapter Seventeen

Roadmaps for Success

"Commitment leads to action. Action brings your dreams closer."

Marcia Wieder

Whether you teach surgeons techniques in the evaluation of acute trauma victims or kindergartners the alphabet you succeed or struggle based on your approach to the material. All outstanding teachers pay particular attention to the fine details of how the course material is developed. These efforts at development can pay dividends for students in many ways.

My approach starts with a decision about what the picture will look like if the student succeeds. In the case of the surgeon I would hope that at the end of the course they would be highly competent in the evaluation of trauma victims and can practice independently at a high level in any hospital that receives such patients. For the kindergartners the picture would be one where they all can sing the alphabet forward and backward, smiling as they do it.

This approach, pioneered by Stephen Covey in the Seven Habits of Highly Successful People, directs us to begin with the end in mind. If the end is student competence or mastery of a course of study or a lesson plan then by visualizing, brainstorming, and defining what that "looks like" then we have a good starting point. Additionally, this can be done for almost any course of study.

It may seem trivial or self evident but if we stop and try to visualize what that idealized outcome looks like then we are perfectly framed to create a map to get there. The two most important way-points on a journey such as this are (1) where we want to be if everything goes well, and (2) where we are right now. The outstanding teacher can tell you those two points for any student under their supervision at any given time.

Once we know the starting and the finishing point then we are in a position to create a roadmap for the student's success. We do that by breaking the material into segments and directing mastery of the segment. This is a process that is individualized to each student ideally. The segments can be broken into bites and the bites can be broken into morsels. Outstanding teachers know how to do this. Exemplary teachers do this and add value by making the morsels delicious.

Let's see how this works in real usage. I recently taught a seminar on Ernest Hemingway and his role in American literature. As you know he was awarded both the Pulitzer Prize and the Nobel Prize in literature and is regarded as among of the most important writers in American history. My students came from all kinds of backgrounds. Some knew more about Hemingway than I did and some had never read anything by him. Most fell in between. At the outset of the class I asked everyone what they hoped to get out of our time together. I wanted to brainstorm on a consensus of goals if there was one. From there we decided that at the end of the session that "ideally" all the students would gain proficiency in three areas. First, everyone would have completed the reading list of short stories and novels representative from his early, middle, and later periods. Second, each student would have a good understanding of the biographical information on Hemingway, his family history, his life experiences, and how these may have influenced his work. And lastly, each student would have a good understanding of the scholarly analysis and criticism of Hemingway and how it evolved over the last seventy-five or so years.

So now that we had an idealized goal we could work backward from it to create a series of paths for success. For those who already knew Hemingway well the path would be different from those who where uninitiated. We wanted the course to be fun and valuable for both. For the content section we read out loud in class. Hemingway is well suited for a readers group and all the students liked it. For the biographical information we used a Problem Based Learning method (more about this in future chapters) where we divided things up into morsels such as his timeline, his father, his mother, his wives, places he lived and we each took a morsel. That way everyone had a chance to contribute in class. This worked particularly well. As far as the scholarly analysis this is where the most experienced students took the lead. I assigned them to go over analysis and writing by college professors and to tell the group whether or not they agreed with them. In conclusion, we were able to integrate the needs of a disparate group of students, master the material and have fun.

The exemplary teacher creates roadmaps to success by beginning with the goal, understanding the starting point, building segments, and morsels. She then tries to make the morsels as tasty as possible. This works over and over again.

Chapter Eighteen

The Process-Focused Teacher

"Practice yourself in little things, and thence proceed to greater."

Epictetus

Exemplary teachers are "process-focused". They benchmark goals to process. They rethink process with an eye toward improvement. They are willing to try different processes. They monitor outcomes and celebrate success, but they are primarily focused on process. Exemplary teachers know that a strict focus on process will produce the best outcomes over time and they are confident of that fact. Outcomes are the results of many factors. Sometimes these factors are outside of our control. Process looks at factors that are within our control.

So what is all this talk about process and outcome? What are processes and what are outcomes? How do we measure and influence each? What are the differences between the two and how do we set up benchmarks to measure them? All good questions, and for those who are not versed in "systems engineering" I will go over some of these concepts in some detail. For those of you who know the techniques of six sigma or rapid cycle process improvement please bear with me.

When I worked at a community hospital in charge of quality improvement one of the many things we measured was what percentage of our elderly patients were up to date on their flu vaccines at the time of hospital discharge. We knew from comparing our baseline data to comparative data from other hospitals in our state, region, and nation that we were doing fairly well but we could be doing better. We looked at data from the top performing hospitals and decided we wanted to benchmark against them. As you know elderly who receive the flu vaccine are less likely to get influenza, less likely to be re-admitted to the hospital for all reasons, and less likely to die of complications of medical or surgical diagnoses. So we had good reason to benchmark off of best hospital data.

First we chose one unit on our hospital. Then we collected baseline data by simply looking at the next 50 or so patients who came to the unit and determined if at discharge they were up to date on their flu shot. This represented our starting batting average. Then we formed a team of nurses, clerical people, doctors, social workers, caseworkers, and pharmacists. As a team we did the following things. First, we created a goal statement. It read something like this: "On unit such and such we will increase influenza vaccines to 90% of all eligible patients by such and such specific date". As you can see our goal statement is precise, time limited, and easily measured.

Then as a group we met and made of flow diagram of the elderly patient's path through the particular unit with respect to the influenza vaccine. A number of issues came up. When does the patient get asked about vaccination status? What if they don't remember? Who orders the vaccine? How does the vaccine get to the patient? And so on. We were able to generate a pictorial map of where all the critical steps were in the process of coming to the unit and the likelihood of getting vaccinated. Remember, none of these patients were admitted for vaccination. They were admitted for other reasons. Then our group met and brainstormed about ideas that might improve the likelihood of getting a vaccination. As a group we rank ordered which of the interventions (we had a long list) were the most likely to show improvement and were the easiest to implement. System engineers call these steps “high-leverage interventions”. Then we would try the new intervention and measure all the patients on that unit for a week. The next week we would try a new intervention and measure the results after it.

As we were doing this project we measured data and plotted on a simple run graph so we could show time along the x-axis and percentage vaccinated along the y-axis. The interventions were simple things like a poster to educate the doctors, or a red sticker that went on the chart to remind the nurses to vaccinate, or an instruction sheet for the clerk to call the physician’s office. Probably the most helpful thing we did was to move a number of the vaccinations to the refrigerator on the unit, rather than in the pharmacy so the nurses had ready access to them when needed.

Needless to say our little project showed a great improvement in our vaccine success and we quickly moved to percentages well above state, national, and even top performing hospitals. Using systems engineering in process improvement to drive quality outcomes is perfectly suited for the educational setting. I have given seminars going over this approach in much greater detail for teachers and educational leaders and they have gone on to use these techniques to drive marked improvement in their classrooms and school districts. These techniques are easily mastered by anyone. They are very powerful and they are fun. They draw from teachings in "Six Sigma" and "Rapid Cycle Quality Improvement". I would encourage anyone interested to look into these areas further.

Let me give one more example of a "Rapid Cycle Quality Improvement" project in an educational setting that I was involved with. A school district consulted me because the sixth graders in one of its poorest schools were reading well below grade level. First we assembled a team of school administrators, teachers, and reading specialists. We decided that we would work with only ten students in the sixth grade. We established a baseline reading level of second grade for eight of the students and third grade for two of the students. Then we constructed our goal statement. It was precise, time specific, and measurable. As a group we developed a flow chart of the process of reading and reading comprehension for students who were behind. Then we brainstormed for ideas that might help these kids. Some were simple. Some were complex. Some were costly. Some were cheap. Some were easy to implement. Some we felt were good ideas but difficult to implement. Then we prioritized which would get us the most leverage and we rank ordered them. Going into these brainstorming sessions I think that most of us thought that no new ideas would come out of our sessions but I think we were all surprised. We tried seven interventions in 6 months and at the end of the time all students had advanced in reading and seven out of ten had advanced to grade level. In our experience the interventions which were most helpful were (1) one extra 40 minute session one on one with reading tutor three times weekly and (2) reading out loud with follow up query for comprehension in small groups. Our interventions and results may not be helpful or cost effective for all environments but that is the point. You have to do what works best in your own environment. In the setting described the process worked well and was very constructive. I am involved in a number of similar projects currently throughout the country involving rapid cycle quality process improvement. I would recommend that all educators learn as much as they can on this subject and get involved in projects like this at their school and classroom level.

Exemplary Teachers are Process Improvement Specialists. They understand the principles of Rapid Cycle Process Improvement and are involved in them in their classrooms and on their campuses.

Chapter Nineteen

Process-Focused Success Stories

"Every time you wink the stars move." Emerson

Success from process improvement projects strengthens the abilities of all exemplary teachers. Even the smallest of projects can totally turn a classroom around or solve a sticky problem. In the beginning it is important to select a project with a reasonable goal and a small enough scale so that it is manageable. The key thing is to start small and build on small and frequent success.

One project that I am familiar with involved teaching elementary school students state capitals. The goals were modest. After establishing a baseline where the students were right about twenty percent of the time the teacher and her students defined the problem and made a goal statement of increasing competence to fifty percent. In order to make a good goal statement it needs to be time-limited and measurable. So the class decided to set a time of three months and decided that they would have a quiz every Friday (measurable). The progress was tracked on a run chart that was displayed at the front of the class. As I described in the last chapter the run chart has time (weeks 1-12) on the bottom (x) axis and the percentage (0-100%) on the up and down (y) axis. Therefore progress was made when the line was moving higher over time. Since the goal was fifty percent a large red line was drawn parallel to the (x) axis at the 50% mark.

Then the class met with the teacher for a brainstorming session on ways to build a higher group score on the state capitals. There were some good suggestions. Then the group decided which interventions they wanted to try first, second, etc. The plan was to have a new intervention each week starting on a Monday with a measurement on a Friday.

From the beginning the project had buy-in from the students and the teacher. And as you can imagine the cumulative scores went up each week. Many of the interventions were successful but one that was particularly noteworthy was when the students designed and constructed "flash cards" with the state on one side and the capital on the other. These cards were very well done, some better than others, and some almost collectible. They were used to practice with in and outside of class and some were even traded. After the flash cards where conceived and built the Friday score went up dramatically. At the end of this small project the class exceeded their goal by achieving a cumulative score of 90%. In this class the teacher took this process improvement project one step further and created a "Story Board" that mapped out what was done and how the results were changed. Remarkably, the students became the ambassadors of this project and later in the year the teacher and her class were recognized for their good work.

My question is simple. Do you think that after the success that this teacher achieved on this State Capitals Project she met enthusiasm when she considered another process improvement project? Further, do you think that the word of mouth regarding this teacher is favorable or unfavorable?

All exemplary teachers leverage their process improvement skills to stimulate learning and enthusiasm.

Chapter Twenty

The Loudest Sound of All

"A wise man learns from the mistakes of others, a fool by his own."

Latin Proverb

Although nobody likes to discuss it because it seems self- evident but "actions do speak much louder than words". Everyday in settings all around the world near and far people study others actions and make decisions based on them rather than on what they say. Teachers almost always profess to be aware of this but in reality it is a lesson that we need to learn over and over again.

Some time ago when I was a physician working in an emergency room I wrote some papers on improving patient communications and one of the things I stressed was letting patients have a chance to tell you their issues before you interrupt them. It is important to be a good listener to be a good communicator I said in my article. Later I said the same thing in lectures to students, residents, and some talks I gave to other doctors. At a later date and for a different project the physicians in our group were being videotaped in our emergency room interacting with patients. When I reviewed the video of my interaction I could see that I was constantly interrupting patients before they finished telling me what was wrong. This was a wake up call to better monitor my actions. After all actions speak louder than words.

In the medical arena doctors who smoke counsel us to quit. Doctors who are overweight counsel us to diet. Doctors who are sedentary counsel us to exercise. What is the message here? In the classroom and at the teacher-learner interface learners are acutely aware of the teacher's actions. In interviews after a classroom lecture students may not remember the teacher's lesson but they are sure to remember the teacher's actions. Was the teacher nervous? Was the teacher cross? Did he bluff knowledge when a question was asked? You name it. When it comes to actions students are incredibly perceptive.

Any teacher with any experience will tell you that students learn very quickly how to push their buttons. Teacher's buttons are sensitivities and anxieties that are vulnerabilities that can be brought out in the teacher-learner interface. When words and actions are not totally in harmony learners pick up on this right away. Learners are extremely sensitive to disharmony in the language behavior dimension.

This disharmony can manifests in so many ways. Perhaps a few examples would be helpful in understanding the process. Students always judge how well the teacher knows the subject. In this regard it never makes sense to "fudge" an answer to a question. In a small experiment we asked teachers who were experts in art and art history to meet with a group of beginning students. Among the students was a "plant" who asked a very difficult question about an obscure artist from the mid seventeenth century. We videotaped the teachers responding to the question. In all cases the other students could tell if the teacher was fudging the answer even if they didn't know the answer themselves. Also the teachers who answered honestly and said they didn't know or that they weren't certain were much more highly rated by the students than those who tried to "bluff" the answer.

In another example of the harmony of words and actions if the teacher sets out a schedule, limit, boundary, or due-date, and then changes it without an adequate explanation students are likely see the words don't equal actions outcome and the next time a schedule or boundary is set the learners might be suspicious. At all levels of learning students access words verses actions.

The core observation that all learners quietly dissect is the answer to a simple set of questions: Why is this teacher teaching this class? Why here? Why now? Why is he teaching me? All learners come to a conclusion on these questions. The most important inputs to the formation of that conclusion are teacher behaviors, not teacher words, or teacher lessons. If the teacher doesn't want to be in the class, doesn't love the subject, or doesn't believe in the students, learners will pick up on it immediately.

Exemplary teachers work to align word and action, and knowing that their actions are more important than their words they work diligently to improve the harmony of the two.

Chapter Twenty-One

A Simple Act that will Change a Life

"We can do no great things, only small things with great love."

Mother Teresa

Some time ago I gave a number of workshops on improving communication skills for physicians and learned a lot of interesting things from the process. We are all resistant to change the way we do things even when we logically know that the change will do us good. Physicians, in my opinion, can be among the most resistant to change in this way. After I received some positive feedback for my work I started to receive physician learners who were sent to my seminars because of transgressions or patient complaints about their interpersonal communication skills. These "mandated" participants were often strongly resistant to change but on a positive note when we did pry them onto a slightly different path their growth was the most durable. Additionally the most hardened initial participants often became the most ardent cheerleaders once they were converted.

Most of the doctors in my groups were basically sound in terms of their knowledge base and skill sets (if you remember the four-legged stool analogy from earlier chapters) and were not evaluated for "citizenship" in these sessions but arrived because of a desire or need to improve communication skills. I talk about doctors because these are the students that I had. I think that these principles apply to accountants, ice hockey coaches, or second-grade teachers equally well.

My message to the doctors, or the hockey coaches, or the second-grade teachers is the same: The lesson that you give, or the actions that you take, or the bones that you set are not complete unless there is some karmic transfer. It can be infinitesimally small or gigantic but this dimension must be served. You can imagine the response that I got from a room full of crusty doctors when I started to talk about "karmic transfer" as the fundamental basis of communication. As a matter of fact I don't think anybody likes the concept at the outset- but in my opinion it is one of the most important secrets of great communication.

Let me start by giving an example from my own life that seemed to resonate with the surgeons who attended my sessions. By the way I always loved working with surgeons and they generally make excellent communicators. They are also excellent students and they generally love to focus on a task until they master it. In my younger days I owned an old but loved German sports car. I could afford a newer one but I was particularly attached to the one I had. I loved to drive it on a summer day or on a weekend. I loved to take it on trips to the lake or into the country. The car was special to me. And it was also temperamental. There seemed to be always something that needed to be adjusted, repaired, or replaced. Fortunately these issues were usually minor. There were two mechanics in my town that provided this kind of service and both were competent and reasonable. Let me tell you how they differed and why I am telling you this story. The first mechanic would simply diagnose the problem, fix it competently, and bill me fairly. He was courteous, timely, and did what he promised. What more could I ask for you say? The second mechanic did everything the first mechanic did but then would take me into the shop and we would have a discussion something like what follows.

"Doctor, I've fixed that squeaking sound that your brakes were making. Do you have a minute to see something?"

"Yes, certainly." I would say. We walked into the work area where one of the front and rear wheels was still off the car. Then he pointed to the front and rear brakes that he had worked on, and spoke.

"I loved what they have done with the 1965 model. Look at the size of those calipers. You certainly have a nice machine here even thirty-five years after its build date. Promise me you will take good care of it."

"Thank you. I will."

"If you walk up front I will snap these wheels back on and meet you outside. Did you have any questions?"

"No. I'm good."

Then he would carefully drive my old car out front with a big smile his face and hand me the keys.

Now let me ask you the same question that I ask in my seminar: All things being equal which mechanic would you prefer? Aside from a few disruptive learners most preferred the second mechanic. Why? Because he seemed to take an interest in us and our problem and he showed a love and appreciation for something that, although small, might be important to us. This is what I am talking about when I say "karmic transfer". By the way I did exclusively use the same mechanic for many years and was always satisfied.

So lets bring it into the realm of the surgeon, the hockey-coach, or the second-grade teacher: Is the patient healed when the diagnosis is made and the problem is solved mechanically? Is mastery obtained when the hockey player demonstrates that she can shoot a slap shot from the blue line? Has a second-grader progressed when he can read out loud at grade-level? I say no one is totally healed, no goal is actually scored, and no academic accomplishment is made until there is some small "karmic transfer".

"Tommy. We took out your appendix last night and I think you should be feeling much better. I will be monitoring you closely. By the way when I was operating inside your belly last night your muscles and everything else looked really good. Did you have any questions?"

"No. Thank you, doctor."

"Julie. I am really pleased by how well you are cracking that slap shot. I know you are going to score a lot of goals. If you continue to work hard the sky is the limit for you in hockey. I think you love playing as much as I used to."

"Thanks coach. I'll keep practicing."

"Billy. Your reading in class is really improving. It seems like you enjoy reading out loud. That is a really good sign. Keep up the good work."

"Yeah. I was nervous at first but now I kind of like it."

"Well, I'm not surprised. You have a very strong voice."

There is so much to improving communication skills and the feedback that we give as teachers is so important to our learners. Even the most talented and gifted surgeon lights up when she gets a pat on the back after successfully learning a small concept in a role playing exercise. It is marvelous to see and refreshing to know that we can all grow our knowledge and abilities.

The first step in improving communication is to think about small "karmic transfers". Hopefully this will remind us that it is not enough to teach to mechanical or robotic competence. It is always best to teach to the mind and the heart. Teaching to mechanical competence is the first step. The second step is to "teach to joy". This can be accomplished by incorporating small "karmic transfers".

Exemplary Teachers know how to create joy in the subject and its mastery. They know how to transfer this joy to the learner. They traffic in "Karmic Transfers".

Chapter Twenty-Two

Moving to a Learner-Centric Model

"The more I want to get something done, the less I call it work."

Aristotle

When I attended school long ago someone far away designed the curriculum, the lesson plan, the teacher's notes, the testing and evaluation materials. As a student I often wondered what those "far away" people were thinking? How in the world could they make such an interesting topic so dull? Of course I had some maverick teachers who said: "Wait a minute this is an important and interesting topic and I want to teach it in a way that differs from the central planners." And they went off on their own and at what peril I am not certain but I thank them very much although belatedly.

The public school system has retained a lot of the "far away" central planning and it gains and slips through time but is generally traceable to funding sources. The old saying goes something like this: "He who pays the piper calls the tune." And the arguments for and against local and distant design of the learning path are the subject of entirely different forum with strong feelings on both sides. My view is for local control as long as outcomes are favorable. I understand the distant control point of view. Nevertheless I do not want to focus on minimum standards. "Minimum standards" is where the so-called experts live and focus their energies. This is where the "far away control" crowd spends their energy. What I prefer to focus on is quite different. I am talking about what is "exemplary", and there is no doubt that "exemplary" means local design, local flexibility, and local assessment. So maybe there is no argument. If we want a system whose goal is a minimum for everyone central planners wave your flags. If you want to go from good to great or beyond then hold onto your local control.

The learner-centric model is simple. It is a model that revolves around the needs of the learner. It assumes that all learners are unique in many aspects. They learn in certain ways. They have unique needs and concerns, and their goals differ from one individual to the next. Think of many paths to the mountaintop. Some are better than others given time, pace, hiker ability, and weather. The way that we assess our learner's needs and concerns is simple, we ask! It seems easy enough but attend any lecture, presentation, seminar, public or private school, undergraduate or graduate course or program and focus on one thing: Does the professor ask what the needs and concerns of the students are? Is the teacher knowledgeable and responsive to the needs of the pupils? Or, as I am certain you will find in over 90% of your observations, the needs are assumed.

It is such a simple thing probing for needs, but who does it? Almost nobody. We assume needs. But people's needs are unique and not always what we think they are. Probing for needs may make an ordinary teacher extraordinary. Let's look at a few examples. When I was a full time teacher of resident physicians I strongly advocated a patient-center approach to medical care. This approach has gained some acceptance over the years but there continues to be resistance by many in medicine despite its effectiveness and humaneness.

Consider the elderly patient who lives alone and who has fallen and fractured her hip. We know because we are knowledgeable and skilled physicians that the best course of care for her is to stabilize her for surgery and take her to the operating room and fix her fracture. Also we get rehab involved as well as nutritional support and her medical doctor to manage her medical issues pre and post op. When we bring the consent form we explain what our plans are and she signs. Everything goes well and on the third day post op she is transferred to a rehab unit. In our mind everything has gone according to plan and she has gotten the best possible result. Right? No, wrong!

We didn't ask her about her needs and concerns. In my classes I mandated that all my residents put their hand on their patient's shoulder and ask clearly and slowly: What are your needs and concerns? This is one of the key questions of a patient-centered model. It starts the dialogue that includes the patient in her care. It aligns the doctor and patient. It is one of the most important questions that a professor can ask her students, a parent can ask her children, a counselor can ask her clients. I can't tell you how many times after I have asked someone about their needs and concerns they have expressed surprise and said. "Gee, that is the first time someone has asked me what my needs are? Wow! That feels incredible."

In the patient-centered model there is no promise of a solution, but there is a promise of understanding the patient's needs and concerns. If we had asked the elderly patient what her needs and concerns were at the time of her hospitalization it might have gone something like this:

"Mrs. Jones, you have a badly fractured hip and I think it is your best interest to have it repaired in the operating room, that way you will have the best chance of a good recovery. Can I go over the risks and benefits of this course of treatment with you in detail."

"Sure, doctor."

"Ok, but before I do I know that everyone is different so I just wanted to take a moment to ask you specifically what are your needs or concerns?" He sits by her bedside and reaches his hand to her shoulder.

"Thank you doctor. I really appreciate that. You know I totally trust your judgment and that if I need an operation I want you to do it. My main issue is silly really. You know I live at home by myself and my old dog Mickey is there alone. I just love that dog and right now there is no one to check on him, to feed him, or to take him for a walk. I am really worried about him. I'm a tough old goat and I'll be Ok, but I don't know what to do about my dog."

The doctor smiles and takes in a deep breath. "I feel the same way about my dog Scalpel. Let me call social service and see if we can arrange something to help you out here. If not my wife knows a few dog sitters we might try."

"Oh, thank you doctor. I can't tell you how much better that makes me feel." A small tear forms in her eye. As it turns out social service arranges for a neighbor to help out with the dog. She is glad to do it for the elderly lady. The surgery goes well and on a survey form the patient writes. "I was treated very professionally and they met all of my needs. I highly recommend the doctor, staff, and hospital."

This is just one example of how a patient-centered approach can work. In the same way we need to always be thinking "learner-centric" in the courses that we teach and the lessons that we give. Like the elderly patient with the fractured hip learners have unique needs and if they are given the opportunity to voice them it encourages "buy-in" and appreciation. Let's go through a few simple examples. A college professor is teaching a seminar on the Seven Americans who have won the Nobel Prize for Literature. At the beginning of the seminar he briefly explains his plan, goals, and reading list and he asks each student to take five to ten minutes to write down their needs and concerns with regard to this course and his stated plan. He is surprised to learn that there are a number of constructive suggestions most of which are easy to implement. They range from a student with a slight hearing problem that requests a seat closer to the front of the room to a request to include in the syllabus the history of the Nobel Prize and how it came to be.

After this assignment one student stops the professor and thanks him for asking about "needs and concerns". He really appreciates it and none of his other teachers are as thoughtful as he is.

Some time ago I was asked to consult with a college professor who was struggling with his teaching skills. He was a brilliant researcher and very knowledgeable in his specialized field of economics. He was well regarded by his peers and colleagues but got low ratings from his students on his teaching skills. This had caused him great anxiety and he had volunteered to have me come in and look at his processes and make suggestions. I enjoyed working with him. I attended a number of his courses and listened carefully to what he hoped to accomplish by working with me. We reviewed his student evaluations together. I wanted to know what his needs and concerns were.

We decided that we were going to gradually evolve his teaching style to a learner-centric model. At the beginning of every course he would probe for student needs, concerns, and suggestions. At the beginning of every class he would ask the students to write suggestions, concerns, or needs on a standard form that he created. Then, weekly, we carefully reviewed the student comments. Strangely most of the comments were positive and the others were constructive and helpful. He took the suggestion of not simply grading the homework and moving on but rather going over each of the questions until there was understanding. He took the suggestion to come out from behind the podium and to sit closer to the students. He took the suggestion to smile more and to praise the students who spoke up in class and tried to answer the question whether correctly or not. He took the suggestion to ask those in the back if they could hear him. He took the suggestion to lecture less and go over problems more. And so by creating a learner-centric model he created a constant feedback loop for improvement.

I knew that he wanted to improve or his university would not have sought me out. I knew that he had the knowledge and skills to do an excellent job but he just needed a system to implement. We did a number of other things during our time together so I cannot say that his changed student evaluations are totally from the learner-centric approach but within a semester he began to get very high ratings from his students. These high ratings have been durable and have created a virtuous cycle in which his dread of teaching has become a joy that he looks forward to everyday.

Exemplary teachers use a learner-centric model and constantly focus on learner needs, concerns, and suggestions. They understand how important this feedback is, and work to make improvements based on it.

Chapter Twenty-Three

More Learner-Centric Skills

"We must not, in trying to think about how we can make a big difference, ignore the small daily differences we can make which, over time, add up to big differences that we often cannot foresee."
Marian Wright Edelman

The second key concept in the learner-centric model is really an extension of the first. Simply put, before starting a new course, lesson, or path it is important to get agreement from all the learners on the goal. This can be done formally in writing or preferably informally simply by asking. For example the teacher might say something like: "This week we are going to review some of the early short stories of Ernest Hemingway as well as what was going on in his life at the time he was writing them. So, if we are successful each of you will be able to argue how the author was projecting his own issues onto his work at this time. Does everyone agree with this week's goals and plan?"

Generally speaking when given the opportunity to approve a goal most people will. But the second part to this concept is that if there is not total acceptance then the key is to "negotiate for mutual agreement". These two parts are powerful in education not only because they align the work of the teacher and the learner but more importantly they create "buy in" from the learner. Research has shown that students who agree in advance to goals they have helped design are much more likely to work toward the goals achievement than those who have not.

Negotiating for mutual agreement doesn't mean necessarily making unacceptable changes to a course rather it simply means taking the input of the learners into consideration. Let me give you an example.

Teacher: "This month students we are going to learn about the presidents from 1900 to 1950. Is everyone OK with that goal?"

Class Clown: "I would rather learn about the baseball players from 1900 to 1950."

Teacher: "That's a good suggestion, Jason. Would you like to do a special report on which baseball teams each president favored."

Class Clown: "I could try."

Teacher: "Great. Does anyone have any needs, concerns, or suggestions with regard to this plan?"

Another Student: "I'd like to learn about their wives, and families."

Teacher: "OK. Good suggestion."

And so you get a feel for the process. There is a give and take in which the learners are given an opportunity to have input on the plan and the goals. Sometimes the plan is mandated, or can't be altered, and if that is the case so be it. It seems to me that there is always room to make accommodations to student needs, concerns, and suggestions. And if you can't, at least you are trying. This sends a very powerful message to your learners.

When I teach the learner-centric model the objections I hear are fairly consistent. Often teachers say that they don't have time for needs, concerns, and suggestions. They say that the plan is the plan and if the learners don't like it too bad. They say that they are not a nanny or a hand-servant and if the learners want special treatment find another teacher. This is sort of an extreme view but it contains a lot of the objections that I hear in this area. I think that it reflects two things that are worth considering. First, change is difficult even if it is for the better. If you are not used to teaching a learner-centric model it is definitely a change and a period of adjustment is in order. Second, it really doesn't take that much additional time to ask the simple questions that I have outlined. Actually it often saves time because there may be certain aspects of the curriculum that are not necessary for class, if everyone agrees.

The second major objection I hear is that the curriculum is designed in advance, or is cast in stone, or cannot be changed without the approval of the department chairperson, superintendent, or grandmother-in-law. Nothing is cast in stone. All teachers have some leeway in teaching. And seeking student input is a positive in itself. I know a teacher that once said to a student. "You know I agree with you suggestion but I am not able to make those changes. I will pass on you suggestions to my department chairperson." That statement in itself is a positive interaction.

And the third objection I get when suggesting a learner-centric approach is the most troubling. This is the one that goes something like this. "These students are ungrateful and don't deserve any special approach. The course is taught the same today as last year and will be the same next year. In other words like it or lump it." I don't have a specific response here other than to say that teaching can be frustrating and unrewarding. Sometimes the frustration that we feel is unconsciously directed toward our learners. We need to be on high alert to avoid the "us verses them" mentality. Additionally, these kinds of comments are "red flags" that other issues may be present.

The exemplary teacher focuses on a learner-centric approach and strives to get agreement on the goal of the course or the lesson. Part of this process involves negotiating for mutual gain.

Chapter Twenty-Four

A Pneumonic for a Learner-Centric Approach.

"Optimism is the faith that leads to achievement, nothing can be done without hope and confidence." Helen Keller

"If I keep a green bough in my heart, the singing bird will come." Chinese Proverb

The "learner-centric approach" is critical to achieving extraordinary success as a teacher, in my opinion. Asking about needs, concerns, and suggestions can align students with teachers and create a positive foundation for learning. Agreeing on goals and negotiating for a mutually acceptable plan to achieve those goals is helpful in the same way. I am always amazed by the difference it makes if the students are "bought in" to the goals, path, and approach verses traditional methods where the students simply show up and receive the lesson passively. This is like comparing lightning to the lightning bug. If you want your classroom to be transformed give the idea of a learner-centric approach at try.

An easy to remember pneumonic that I use in the learner-centric model is "IOU". "IOU" keeps us focused on three key precepts of teaching success. "I" stands for individualize your approach. We all know that learners have differing needs and concerns and by accommodating them when possible you are doing a wonderful thing. Remember to probe for needs, concerns, and suggestions, simply ask. Create a mechanism for the learner needs to reach you either in writing or in person. Once you know about learner needs it is important to acknowledge them and, when possible, accommodate them.

"O" stands for optimism. Optimism is powerful. Optimism is contagious. Optimism is transformative. Whether you are teaching senior citizens how to power up their Ipads and surf the Internet or you are teaching English as a second language in a remote region of Thailand you need optimism. When a learner senses your optimism she progresses faster and higher and will exceed goals. Optimism creates virtuous cycles in learning. Let me give you a few examples and see if you don't agree that optimism is crucially important.

When I was twelve my father paid for me to have guitar lessons. I wanted to learn to play guitar but it did not come easily to me. I followed my instructor's plan and completed all of my assigned practice sessions. My instructor seemed frustrated with my progress. He did not seem optimistic about my future as a guitar player. After about the fifth lesson when my dad came to pick me up the instructor sat me in the hall and brought my dad around the corner out of my sight. But it was quiet in the hall and I could hear them talking. The instructor told my dad not to waste any more money on guitar lessons for me. And that was it. To this day I would like to play a musical instrument but I am uncomfortable about trying again.

On the other hand I observed a swim teacher who taught adult swimming classes. The students were beginners and most could not swim at all. Some had serious health problems. Others had had prior bad experiences and failures in learning to swim. At the beginning most of the adults felt clumsy and fearful. I watched some of the early sessions and then interviewed the teacher. In the beginning it did not look good for the students. Some didn't even want to get in the water. Others were hopelessly uncoordinated. One elderly woman swallowed a mouthful of pool water and wanted to give up. The teacher would have nothing of it. When I spoke to the swim teacher she had a calm confidence about her. I asked her if she thought any of these adults could learn to swim. She told me that she was confident that they all could. I asked her how she could be so optimistic and she told me it was her nature. She asked me to think of the best swimmer that I know and remember that she was once a clumsy beginner. That thought stuck with me. Her optimism was contagious.

I returned to the pool six weeks and then twelve weeks later. None of her students in this class had given up. And at twelve weeks the elderly woman who had swallowed water and wanted to give up was swimming laps and working her way up to swimming one mile without stopping. She seemed transformed. I asked her how she was able to progress so well when it seemed likely she would fail or quit. The elderly woman smiled and told me that she had a teacher that believed in her. That optimistic approach made all the difference. I couldn't agree more.

The third letter in IOU is "U". "U" stands for "under promise". For learners to be virtuously reinforced it is important for them to meet or exceed their goals. If we promise too much we struggle to meet them. Even if we do well by an objective measure we may not meet expectations. Performance verses expectations means everything to a student. It is important to let students meet or exceed their goals before we set new ones.

The swim teacher in my last example did not promise that she would make championship swimmers out of the beginners. What she did promise is that if her students would commit to trying their best she would help them make progress. And she always did. Also promises should always focus on process, not outcomes. Outcomes can be affected by factors outside of our control. Processes are mostly within our control. So, for example, the swim teacher never promised that the students would swim a mile nonstop within a year- although many set that as their long term goal. What she promised is that she would commit her best efforts and experience to focus on building the skills necessary in her swimmers to meet their goals. This turned out to be an under-promise because she always did more.

So try to remember "IOU" when you are teaching and if you are so inclined in life in general. Individualize your approach based on needs, concerns, and suggestions. Remember that your optimism helps your learners immensely. And when you under-promise you will become trustworthy and reliable in the eyes of your students.

The Exemplary Teacher uses the pneumonic "IOU" to remember to individualize her approach, to be optimistic about her student's progress, and to under-promise so that goals can be reasonably met.

Chapter Twenty-Five

Passive Learning verses Active Learning

"I hear, and I forget. I see, and I remember. I do, and I understand." Chinese Proverb

The most important thing we can do as teachers is to engage our students. The teacher who lectures endlessly, even in the "lecture hall" rapidly loses the student's interest. We live in a world of rapid bites of information. We live in a world of give and take. We live in a world of user-defined content. We all know someone who sits in front of the television and clicks through the channels. We all know someone who has the television on, the radio on, is talking on the phone, texting, and surfing the Internet. For these types of individuals sitting for an hour of lecture is difficult.

The best lecturers can inspire us, entertain us, and motivate us. Lecturers can strengthen their presentation with visual aids such as Microsoft's Powerpoint or Apple's Keynote. They can inspire us with their knowledge, skill, and ability. Some teachers can lecture without notes beautifully. But at the end of the day it is a lecture. It will be a long time before lectures leave education. They are a critical aspect of all formal education and they are a core element of University education.

But lectures contain one critical flaw that we must all acknowledge. They by their nature put the student in a position from which it is difficult to learn. The role of the student attending a lecture is passive. Being passive and trying to learn is difficult. The longer one is passive and trying to learn the more difficult it becomes. I have attended a number of lectures where the presenter compounded this flaw even more. Maybe you also have experienced the following. First, lunch is served. Then the speaker is introduced. Then the lights are turned down. Then the PowerPoint slides begin. The font is very small and the lecturer reads from his slides in monotone. You get my drift. At the end of these presentations often people are awakened when the lights are put back on.

So if lectures put the student in a passive role what approaches are superior? For starters any approach that engages the learner. Ideally, learning should be one hundred percent participatory. Next I will show you how you can accomplish this. But if we must lecture what can we do to involve the student? Can the lecturer ask the audience a question? Of course, and a large audience may respond with a show of hands. Can the lecturer ask the audience to take out a piece of paper and write something down? Of course, and if done correctly it will involve the learners.

Guy Kawasaki, the famous author and venture capitalist, advocates a 10/20/30 rule for PowerPoint presentations. Ten is the maximum number of slides, twenty minutes is the maximum lecture time, and thirty is the minimum font size. This makes a lot of sense if you think about learner's abilities in a passive mode. I would recommend that anyone who teaches by lecture to consider the 10/20/30 rule if you want to improve your PowerPoint presentations.

If lectures put the learner in the most passive of modes what are some other teaching approaches to consider? My favorite by far is the "case-based" approach. This is the approach used by many medical and graduate schools of business. I think that Harvard Business School was among the first to use the "case-based" approach to teaching. Simply defined a real or fictional case is presented that raises a number of questions related to the subject material and the teacher asks the question: What would you do?

Let me begin with a few examples of the "case-based" approach. For many years I taught physicians in training. We would meet in the morning and go over the cases from the prior night. The resident who was "on call" would present the patients that she encountered and cared for during the night. As is the standard practice in medicine the resident would present the patient first in terms of the history, then the physical, then the labs and radiology, then the tentative plan, and then the patient's course. As the young doctors presentations evolved I would stop and turn to the other residents and ask: Given what she has told us so far what are you thinking? What questions would you have asked the patient? What tests would you have ordered? You can see how quickly this becomes one hundred percent participatory on the part of the students. And since we let the residents know what did happen to the patient they get instant feedback on their approach. My role is to keep them on course and to give them knowledge that I supposedly have from my years in practice.

In business schools the students read the case that is usually a history of a set of circumstances in a small business or a large corporation. By working through these issues the students confront the problems that companies face and they learn from the decisions and recommendations that they make. By taking the "what would you do and why" approach the learners are immersed in a participatory environment that is highly conducive to learning.

You are probably thinking how could a "case-based" approach apply to my teaching environment? I have found through brainstorming with teachers from all levels and disciplines that "cases" can be created for almost anything.

Cases can be created for first graders and physicists. Cases can be created in social studies and science. Cases can be created in art, music, and literature. Cases can be created in anything. And cases are what invite learners to participate, work through the challenges, and problem solve. Every teacher should develop a set of cases and teach at least part of the time in a "case-based" approach.

Exemplary teachers have a well-developed set of cases and they use these cases to engage their students in problem solving. Exemplary teachers teach "case-based" curriculum.

Chapter Twenty-Six

From Dictator to Facilitator

"The ear of the leader must ring with the voices of the people."

Woodrow Wilson

Consider the track coach. When she leads her team onto the field is she the fastest runner in the group? She is probably not. In the same way does the teacher have to the most knowledgeable person on every aspect of the lesson? It is a great question and one that is debated at many of the seminars that I have been involved with. Traditionally the teacher is the one with all the knowledge and the students are there merely to soak up what bits of knowledge the teacher wants to share. If the educational system is reconstituted slightly into a something dynamic then learners might play a slightly different role. This is the basis of the problem-based approach and this is where the teacher begins to morph from a teacher into a teacher-facilitator. And in case you weren't aware, a teacher-facilitator is a more evolved creature.

Take for example an engineering class. The teacher is discussing cars that are more fuel-efficient. Several questions arise. There are questions about using lightweight materials. There are questions about various propulsion systems, including hybrid-electric. There are questions about tire technologies. In the traditional model the teacher is the expert and in responding to the questions does her best to answer them as completely as she can. However in the new world order the teacher does not reveal her expertise, or lack thereof, but rather acts as a facilitator. The teacher learner exchange goes something like this:

Learner: "Are some metals more suited for cars that are very fuel-efficient? What are the advantages of aluminum as a building material?"

Teacher-Facilitator: "Great question Learner." She goes to the dry erase board and writes: "Advantages and Disadvantages of Various Metals in Building and Efficient

Car." Will you take that question as your assignment for next class and report to us what you have found."

Learner: "Sure. I'll get on the Internet as soon as class is finished."

And so it goes. As the teacher presents on a topic interesting questions or problems arise. The teacher-facilitator lists these problems on the board and assigns them to various learners. At the next session the students report back on their findings. This problem-based learning method brings the subject alive. It involves the students deeply and it flows in the direction that is unique to each student.

In an eighth grade class the learners are watching a video of the presidential inauguration. The teacher-facilitator is making a list of the questions and problems that arise from the class and lists them on the board. Some of them are as follows.

"Seemed like a cold day. Was it the coldest inauguration?"

"How does one get tickets to an inauguration?"

"Is it always on the same date?"

"Why was Aretha Franklin chosen to sing?"

All good questions and probably easily answered by the teacher. But the teacher-facilitator assigned these problems to students in the class that would present their answers on the next day. In this way the students who do a good job get recognized as being "experts" in the area that they researched. This method encourages participation and brings the subject to life.

In "Case-Based PBL (problem-based learning)" the teacher-facilitator leads with a case that is relevant to the subject matter and then dissects it with her learners. As questions arise a "problem list" is created and assigned. At the next meeting there is follow up. This takes Problem-Based Learning (PBL) to the next level. In the seminars that I have been involved with we focus a lot of time on designing and developing cases that work with PBL for all levels of learners. However the teacher as facilitator concept is something that anyone can begin right away.

All exemplary teachers are versed in Problem-Based Learning and are skilled at integrating appropriate and relevant cases into their teaching. Exemplary teachers enjoy the role of the facilitator and draw out participation that transforms learners into problem solvers and researchers.

Chapter Twenty-Seven

Running Down the Horses

"So long as a person is capable of self-renewal, they are a living being." Henri Frederic Amiel

I am told that many horses will ride as long as the rider insists. They will not stop to rest. They will run until they fall over. Likewise when the Native Americans hunted deer they would chase them and then run them until they could flee no more and they were defenseless. The problem was in the beginning the deer would run as hard as possible under the influence of their flight response. This sapped a lot of their energy reserves and under pursuit they would burn up their fuel. Within six to eight miles of hard pursuit even a strong deer is too tired to run further. But wait you ask I am an educator and striving to do a great job, why are you talking about horses falling over and burn out in deer?

I had a friend who was very financially successful and busy. Actually the more successful he became the busier he became. On paper he was very rich but his life was spiraling out of control. He never saw his wife or his family and he was juggling many balls in the air, all at the same time. In many ways his success was controlling him, he was becoming a slave to it, and his quality of life was deteriorating. In his defense he would say things to my like "you've got to strike while the iron is hot."

It all came to a head one day when we were riding in his car. I forget the exact circumstances of our trip but I remember that we were going somewhere in a hurry. The car was a beautiful new European luxury sedan with every option and it had been paid for with cash, but it was a hideous mess inside and out. On the outside there was a coating of road salt, grit, bugs, and mud. You could barely see through the windows in spots. There were a number of minor dings and dents as a result of his carelessness and parking errors. On the inside the dash was covered with reports, letters, and DVDs that needed to be returned. A sack of laundry that was meant for the cleaners covered one rear seat. There was a dog cage on the other. On the floor were used coffee cups, fast food bags, coins, and other garbage. Coffee stains covered one of the front seats. I asked him if he had ever serviced the vehicle or changed the oil and filters. And I wasn't surprised to find that he hadn't although he intended to.

We started discussing his situation and where his life was taking him and I asked him about his renewal strategy. He simply said that there was no time and he would think about it when he got back from his business trip. Then we talked about his car and how nice it was and how much I liked it and what a mess it was. He laughed and agreed and promised to clean it soon. But after some time I decided that he shouldn't clean it. Cleaning it would damage its character. This car, in my opinion, was an exact representation of my friend. The car was a beautiful creation with wonderful design features and capabilities that was treated by its owner like a piece of garbage. And that is what I told him. He smiled and said nothing. But I think it made him think. I know he made a number of positive changes in his life. I don't know if it had anything to do with me.

To some degree we are all driving a late model car in which we refuse to change the oil. Many of us are like horses that will not stop and rest. And some of us are like deer running away and losing our energy. In other words we have not learned how to take care of ourselves. This obsession with work without renewal is deeply seated in our culture and in each of us. And although we understand intellectually that we would be more effective in the workplace and at home if we allowed ourselves renewal, many of us don't or won't take the time to accomplish it.

Steven Covey called it "saw sharpening" in his Seven Habits of Highly Successful People. I like to think of it in a slightly different way. Assume for a minute that we are all "battery powered". We need battery power to be successful in our work and family life. A high "battery charge" makes us feel great, allows us to perform at our full potential and beyond, and allows us to confront challenges in our life in a healthy and productive way. But we confront many "battery drains" in the course of our daily life. Lack of sleep, poor diet, cloudy weather, difficult assignments at work, a problem learner, boredom- everybody's list differs slightly. And everybody can generate a list of "battery drainers". So most of us go through our daily lives on a very low charge. It is just enough to get by but with little in reserve. The sleep that we get and the food that we eat barely holds the "low charge" that gets us from day to day. And that's how many of us live.

So my question to you is the same one I always ask at my seminars: What is your list of things that would fully charge your batteries? When I ask it in this way and we are only talking about ideal actions without limits. One would imagine that this question can generate some pretty interesting answers. But in my opinion the "ideal" is a good place to start. Maybe you would like to generate a list for yourself as we think though this process?

Everybody can come up with renewal activities big and small that would recharge their batteries. And it is important to do this. The next step is critical, however. And that is to implement some of the small ones immediately.

Whether it is walking around the block instead of eating fast food or scheduling a massage once a week start immediately. And once you have started monitor how you feel as you incorporate renewal activities in your life. Monitor how you feel and how you perform. If you are feeling and performing better then the renewal activities are charging your batteries. It is as simple as that.

A teacher that attended a conference where I presented on renewal strategies decided that he would meditate three times a week as his plan to help charge his batteries. Initially it surprised me because he was the school football coach and was a "no nonsense" sort of person, but later I got an email from him saying that his practice has significantly "charged his batteries". So I cannot prejudge what you do for "renewal", but it is critically important that you do it to keep you batteries "charged".

The exemplary teacher has discovered activities and practices that fully recharge her batteries. These

renewal strategies help her performance in all aspects of her life, including teaching.

Chapter Twenty-Eight

Three Words You Need Not Fear

"Good teachers are those who know how little they know. Bad teachers are those who think they know more than they don't know." R. Verdi

I spend a lot of my time in the company of physicians. I have been involved in medicine as a practicing doctor, a teacher of doctors and doctors in training, and as a hospital administrator. And when you spend a lot of time with physicians it is rare to hear the words that I am describing. Actually, for anyone who presents themselves to the world as an expert in his field, whether an auto mechanic or an astronaut, we struggle with the simple phrase that I am referring to.

But to hear it spoken reveals much about the character of the speaker. The phrase, if you haven't guessed already, is "I don't know". It is simple really but to many it reveals weakness. Ask a pilot the maximum carrying capacity of a particular airplane or an expert in literature to tell you about Hemingway's best novel and you will probably get an answer. Ask a doctor if it is better to operate with a scope or by an open method and you will probably get an answer. Ask a teacher what is the best method for teaching kids to read and you will likely get an answer.

But ask someone who has moved beyond the everyday, beyond the surface scratching depths where we usually exist, beyond the simple answers and into the complex and you might get a different response. You might hear what an intriguing question you have posed, one that may need reflection or further study. You may hear in a problem-based approach a suggestion that the learner research the good question further. You might hear the phrase that many experts avoid at all costs, that is: "I don't know."

But what is wrong with "I don't know"? Can we know everything? Are we expected to have anticipated all the questions our learners might ask? Is not knowing a sign of weakness? Can a good question be turned into an assignment for a student or a group of students to solve? Of course it can.

When a well-prepared teacher who is dedicated to the success of her students utters the words “I don’t know”, I find that highly positive. I find it positive because it reveals an inner confidence in the teacher. It reveals an honesty that is sometimes is lacking in discourse. And it also reveals the excitement of the whole educational process. That is, there are a lot of things waiting to be discovered, waiting to be revealed, and waiting to be understood. In this way, saying “I don’t know” is a good first step.

Exemplary teachers are not afraid to say “I don’t know” when a question or problem come up that needs further thought and inquiry. “I don’t know” can be a tool that an exemplary teacher uses as a launching point to further learner inquiry and discovery.

Chapter Twenty-Nine

The Power of Your Beliefs

"You can't direct the wind but you can adjust the sails."

Anonymous

What you believe is more powerful in shaping your destiny and that of your student's than any other single factor. Beliefs can be empowering or crippling, and they are critically important because they dominate how we relate to others. How many times have you heard an educator say that a particular student was "hopeless" or couldn't learn? How many times have we heard a teacher say that the syllabus was poorly designed or the mix of students wouldn't work out? Statements such as these often become self-fulfilling because they emanate from our beliefs and our beliefs are powerful.

For most of us our beliefs are more powerful than obvious facts that contradict them. Sometimes our beliefs fly in the face of all things logical. On the other hand our beliefs can empower us and help us overcome obstacles that logic tells us we shouldn't. Let me give you an example of each circumstance. I once had a friend who lived in a rural community. Nevertheless she was fearful of crime. She watched the news broadcast from far away that reported on crimes in big cities and distant places. The community where she lived in was extremely small and had no criminal activity to speak of. She is a very intelligent person and is a sensible and logical thinker. Yet she never went out after dark. She rarely traveled alone, and at night she locked her apartment with four dead bolts. Over a period of ten years there had been no serious crimes in her community, yet despite these statistics, her behaviors did not change. Her beliefs about the risk of crime were much more powerful than any factual information or experience to the contrary.

On the other hand I know of a woman's field hockey coach who accepted a high school job after the team had losing records for over eleven years. Three years after she started the team played in the State Championship game and has been a good team ever since. When I asked her what she did differently from her predecessors she simply told me that she believed her athletes were capable of winning and convinced them to consider changing their beliefs accordingly. Once they did everything fell into place.

It is critically important for us as teachers to look at our beliefs carefully and ask the question: Do our beliefs empower our learners or hinder them? The answer to this question may be the most important one in education but it is rarely considered. As a student I would much prefer a clumsy teacher who absolutely believed in my success than a talented one who was convinced I would fail. And if you think about it I know that you will agree with me.

We all work in imperfect worlds. Most of the time we don't get to pick our students. Often the teaching materials are inadequate or the environment is substandard for learning or success. There are many obstacles to learning and achievement and they are too numerous to list here but most teachers can quickly state a dozen of them. More important than materials, environment, or other obstacles is our own beliefs about our student's prospects for success. If we believe that our students will do well despite their difficult circumstances they probably will. And if we belief that our students will do poorly because of their circumstances they probably will. What we believe will come true is usually right. The funny thing about beliefs is that we chose them. Please think about that.

The exemplary teacher believes deeply that her learners will excel and are destined for greatness. Additionally, she is constantly monitoring her beliefs for any that may be an obstacle to her teaching success.

Chapter Thirty

First Consultation

"Treat people as if they were what they ought to be and you help them become what they are capable of becoming." Goethe

I have been often asked to evaluate problems or concerns with teachers. Sometimes these consultation result from self referrals, but more likely they are initiated by schools, school districts, universities, and other organizations. In each of these cases I rely on the principles of "Appreciative Inquiry" first described by the great business thinker, David L. Cooperrider of the Weatherford School of Management at Case Western Reserve University in Cleveland. At its core appreciative inquiry begins by looking at what an organization, or individual, is doing well. It focuses on strength first, and relies on the identified strengths to serve as a launching pad for making improvements. I have also found that it reinforces that organizations and individuals tend to minimize their positive attributes when a problem needs to be solved, and starting with a goal of understanding strengths often reorients the process positively.

It has been said many times that there are no shortage of good ideas, but there is definitely a shortage of people who can successfully implement them. This fundamental truth is another key element of projects that I have been involved with. All teachers and those who work with them should strive to add "value" to the processes with which they are involved. Value can be measured and should be benchmarked by what an "ordinary" teacher would do in a particular situation. A "value added" approach occurs if there is a measured positive deviation from ordinary in the process under scrutiny. All exemplary teachers understand this and strive to be "value adders". In the same way a consultation is not successful if only the problem is diagnosed. It is not successful if good ideas or suggestions are made in a report (this, frankly, is the way that over ninety percent of business consultations end). A successful consultation ends when good ideas or suggestions are implemented and value is added in a way that is a measurable improvement from the baseline.

Unfortunately this rarely happens in commercial practice today. Typically the client gets a large bill and a report that says something like: “Dear Customer, We have evaluated your situation and agree that you have the problems that you have identified. Enclosed are some good ideas and suggestions that you might try to improve things. Best of luck in trying to implement them.”

We all know that change is difficult but not impossible. We also know that the tiniest of changes, if they are the right ones, can have dramatic results in helping us achieve the goals that we seek to accomplish or the problems we want to solve. These thoughts serve as an underlying philosophy for me as I approach problems in education. Consultations should not be punitive, rather constructive. And we have the opportunity to grow everyday. So, as Yogi Berra so aptly suggested, “When you come to a fork in the road you should take it.” Ultimately any intervention that is made should be measured for effectiveness, and if we are satisfied that it works, then maybe we should adopt it.

Imagine for a minute that the two of us were called by an educational organization because a teacher is struggling. They have told us what the problem is and have asked us to meet with the teacher and see if we could be of assistance. This is typically the situation in these circumstances. Rarely does the individual self refer for consultation. How should we approach this situation? Let's walk through some broad steps that may be helpful and see if we can learn from them. In this hypothetical approach many of our questions go unanswered and it is the questions that we ask that will guide us.

First, if the organization is asking for help with a particular individual what is the nature of the inquiry? Is there a legal issue or a conduct issue? Is there an alleged boundary violation? Is there a performance or communication issue? With regard to these possibilities it is important to get as specific as possible and it is always important to interview the person asking for the consultation so that their concerns are addressed. As in our learner-centric approach with students it is important to fully understand the needs and concerns of the requester of a consultation so that needs and concerns can be expressed.

Second, let's assume that we have a very clear understanding of what the organization is seeking and it is reasonable then our next step is to meet with the teacher involved. I think it is important to be forthright about the precise issues that the organization is raising and to share those with the individual unless for some reason it is not possible to share the information. This rarely happens in my experience, but if it did I would explain to the individual exactly what my understanding was.

Often people accused of a deficiency will deny it when confronted. It is not my role to adjudicate these issues, rather to share what I know and describe my understanding of the possible benefits of working with me verses the possible risks of not accepting my help. All of that said the goal initially is for all parties to agree on the problem, or the perception of the problem. If this can be accomplished it is a good foundation for a successful resolution. In reviewing cases in which things were not resolved I often find that there was never an agreement on the problem in the first place. Additionally, although I always strive for the best possible outcome for all parties involved I always let all individuals know at the outset who has retained me and why. This is the best way to promote trust from the beginning, in my opinion. If all of this introductory stuff seems adversarial and as it has strayed from what exemplary teachers do bear with me as we walk through these general steps and hopefully it will prove useful for everyday educators.

If we have established agreement on the problem I like to move from the general to the specific. Rather than zero in on this issue that is raised initially I rather look at some overall issues keeping in mind the principles of appreciative inquiry. My first questions are in the realm of: What's going well in the classroom generally? What is going well with regard to the curriculum, student-teacher relations, and student performance? What is going well with regard with your relationship with other teachers, your mentors, and the administration? What is good about this job, the facilities, and your benefits? Along these lines there is a lot of inquiry and the answers are often extremely helpful in understanding the dynamic of the situation. In my experience you rarely have to ask "what is wrong with?" questions. If you ask, "what is going well with" you will hear about the problems and frustrations as well.

Next I like to get a general feel for the four legs of the stool that we talked about in earlier chapters. My questions here relate to Knowledge base, Skill-set, Communication Skills, and Citizenship. By having an honest dialogue in these areas one gets a good understanding of the frustrations, insight, and possible areas to focus or work on.

Then I ask the "belief" questions. These are questions such as: what are your views about the likelihood of success of your learners, curriculum, methods, and processes? These questions if phrased properly can be extremely revealing about an individual and help guide a path for improvement. On one occasion a struggling teacher told me that her school was in a poor neighborhood and she had no belief that anyone entering her class could learn. She saw herself mainly as a baby sitter. While this view may have been widespread, as she suggested to me, my question was how could things ever improve while this belief remained in place. On another occasion I worked with a physician who was accused of violating the boundary rules for his organization by dating his students. His belief was that both he and his student were adults, and therefore the conduct rule wasn't applicable. My question to him was why was the conduct rule written and who was it intending to protect? I am happy to say that in both of these cases both individuals made material changes in their behaviors, felt positive about the changes that they made, and showed dramatic and measurable improvements in their respective areas and in learner outcomes.

So, if the first rule is to apply appreciative inquiry, the second is to agree on the problem, the third to understand the needs and concerns of all stakeholders, especially the individual. The fourth rule is to move from general to specific, then the fifth is to agree on what a successful outcome will look like. If any step in a consultative assignment is more important I don't know of it. Recently I gave a presentation at a convention of high-level consultants who toiled in many industries but were primarily in finance and I told a story about a world champion archer who was introduced to a large audience of learners. The participants were told about the archer in glowing terms, she had won this competition and set this record and from a distance of so many feet she had hit the bull's eye this many times in a row and so on. A target was placed across the auditorium and the archer entered to great applause. Then a blindfold was placed over her eyes. She was pointed in the direction of the target, pulled, fired and totally missed. There was an audible gasp in the room and then commotion. When I returned to the podium I had to tap on the microphone many times before the audience calmed down. Then I told them what I had intended all along: "Even the most talented among us cannot hit a target we do not see."

Think about it, often we are working hard, or frustrated, but what does success look like generally or specifically? Often we don't know. We are all like a champion archer who blindfolded misses the target. If only we could know or have guidance about what we need to do to have success, be exemplary, or, conversely, to get out of a hole, then most of us would simply do it. This is why it is critically important that we ask ourselves: If we are successful in this project, problem, venture, etc what will it look like? This is my favorite question for the organization that asks for my consultation, for the teacher who needs an intervention, for myself if I set out on a project or challenge. It is a question that you might ask yourself. Because if you do then you will be like the archer who takes off the blindfold and sees the target. You will see your goal, understand your task, and get ready to map out your plan. By the way, after the archer takes off her blindfold she routinely hits the bull's eye arrow after arrow much to the delight of the audience who takes home the message transformed.

As suggested in the last paragraph, once we answer the question: if we are successful in this intervention what will it look like, and there is agreement of all stake-holders on the answer, then the final construct is simply a plan. It can be a plan of correction, a strategic plan, a plan of improvement, or any sort of a plan that is appropriate. It must be detailed, time specified, uncomplicated, and measurable. Once the plan is in place and underway the consultant, or other appropriate person, simply encourages, guides, monitors, and keeps the individual on course and on time. Conceptually this is easy, but here is where the good work is done. If the plan is successful the organization is successful, the individual is successful, and those who receive value from the individual are better off. These are all worthy goals. If the effort and desire are there, and these steps are followed, consultations can be very helpful. Not all organizations or individuals can be or should be saved, but these approaches have the best likelihood of success in the appropriate circumstances.

Exemplary Teachers understand the principles of helping other teachers and organizations and apply them in appropriate situations for themselves and their colleagues.

Chapter Thirty-One

Second Consultation

"In education it isn't how much you have committed to memory or even how much you know. It's being able to differentiate between what you do know and what you don't. It's knowing where to go to find out what you need to know and it's knowing how to use the information you get." William Feather

In addition to looking at the challenges faced by individual teachers and helping them make improvements in their approaches to teaching I am often asked to look at organizational issues that revolve around the educational process. In these types of problem solving projects I often use many of the same approaches described in the last chapter. In review: a consultation or intervention is not successful unless a positive measurable change in process or outcome occurs. This occurs by establishing the strengths of the organization with regard to the issue at hand through a process such as "appreciative inquiry". Next there has to be agreement on the problem and agreement on what success looks like, if it can be achieved. After these issues are resolved the usual blocking and tackling of everyday problem solving can occur and be guided in a positive and measurable direction.

The reason that a consultant can be helpful in solving an organizational issue is that the consultant can look objectively at the issues, help build the agreements needed for the foundational work, and guide the stake-holders along a path of improvement. I have seen progress made on intractable problems just by using these simple procedures.

It would be incomplete not to say that organizational dynamics (or dysfunction) is often the biggest impediment to problem solving within groups. Anyone who does organizational consulting at any level knows this, and it can be frustrating. But if momentum is established early, and the foundational agreements are sincerely agreed to in advance those who seek to sabotage progress for whatever reason are often weakened by these deliberative processes.

Some time ago a small liberal arts college needed help in implementing a novel curriculum advance. The school leaders in an effort to improve outcomes for students wanted to require that all freshmen take a writing course. The theory was that better writing improves the communication skills of all disciplines. The problem was that the English Department did not want to take on the burden of teaching extra classes, the administration had only limited resources for additional faculty, and there was a general confusion about how to set up the program.

The discussions that followed led to establishing a number of foundational elements that all the stake-holders agreed upon. First, the concept was a good one. Second, it didn't have to be led by the English Department but they needed to be supportive. Third, it could be developed gradually, over a period of five to seven years with twice yearly retreats to discuss results and make improvements. And fourth, there needed to be a program champion, that is someone who had led a similar program at another organization. First, the important foundational principles were agreed on by everyone, then an enthusiastic champion and bridge-builder was hired, and the program slowly bloomed into one of the best around. Needless to say other colleges are scrambling to catch up on this important curricular advance.

Education, training, development, and growth are key components of any type of organization from small proprietorships to Fortune Fifty corporations, from Religious to Educational organizations. Sometimes they need help in making forward progress on these initiatives. A skilled individual who takes a value-added, results oriented approach can often help organizations get traction on these important initiatives. There is an old saying about paying for a service and it goes like this: "price is what you pay, value is what you get."

Exemplary Teachers are sometimes asked to help their organizations make improvements in processes and outcomes. The precepts outlined broadly in these chapters may serve as a starting point to help in this regard.

Exemplary Teachers are eager to help their organizations improve processes and outcomes. They understand it is important to have a systematic value-added approach that produces measurable forward progress.

Chapter Thirty-two
Third Consultation

"It is the supreme art of the teacher to awaken joy in creative expression and knowledge." Albert Einstein

The third type of consultation, and by far my favorite, is working one on one with learners. The possible gains that can result if the relationship is properly structured are phenomenal. The satisfaction that success presents for the tutor is great, and for the learner there is the possibility of turning a life around. These statements sound like exaggerations, I know, but I have seen it happen over and over and over again. I know there are many great things that can happen on this earth, but one of my favorites, and definitely in the top ten of all things possible is the moment when a motivated learner connects with a gifted tutor. Call me crazy but I feel the "tutor" is the best job there is.

So what are the ingredients that make the tutor-learner relationship work? In many ways they are the same that make the exceptional teacher exemplary. Respect for the individual, mutually agreed upon goals, breaking the curriculum into segments, and then into bites, positive reinforcement, and sincere praise. If you have been reading the prior chapters then you know much about these building blocks. But what are the special characteristics of the learner-tutor relationship that go beyond the classroom?

If you teach in a learner-centric model as we have recommended in prior chapters then you can tutor in a learner-centric model that is laser focused. When you are teaching six to sixty thousand at the same time it is sometimes necessary to make compromises with pace, level of complexity, and content. But in a tutoring situation you can address the exact needs of the learner, and together you can focus with incredible specificity and strength.

I recently had the opportunity to observe one of my former students who was tutoring an inner city student who was flunking math. The learner had a low desire to attend the tutoring sessions initially but the tutor brilliantly worked with his needs and interests to develop and grow a curiosity, modest at first, then almost at the level of a passion. Their session began as follows:

> Tutor: I understand you are struggling with math, is that why you are here?
>
> Learner: No, I am here because I have to be here.
>
> Tutor: Do you like math?
>
> Learner: (Laughing) I hate math?
>
> Tutor: Ok, then, what are you interested in?
>
> Learner: (quietly) Basketball.
>
> Tutor: Great. Could you tell me more about that?

Needless to say basketball is a game with deep ties to math. Free throw percentages, field goal percentages, calculating points per game, vertical leaping ability, and an endless assortment of cases to draw from. From the first day onward the learner worked on mathematical problems that arose from basketball. The bond between tutor and learner was strengthened and the learner's math skills were dramatically improved. I know in this case the pride that the tutor took in his learner's progress was so strong that she started to attend some of the learner's basketball games. Then the learner started to ask questions from his other subjects and his grades overall started to improve. These types of interventions can create a virtuous cycle that has the potential to change a life.

The second key point for tutors to understand is important. Through a careful learner-centric approach you get a glimpse of the problem. The learner is with you for a reason and often a great deal of patience and fortitude is necessary to make one small, forward step. A forward step is always worth patience and fortitude, and it can be the beginning of something good, but learners are stuck for a reason, and getting unstuck is harder than simply pushing off. Let me illustrate this point as follows. When you first learned to swim it was a probably in a very supportive environment. It was safe, you felt reasonably comfortable, and you progressed. The learner who has come before you was taught to swim by being thrown into the cold water and nearly drowning, swallowing water, having to be rescued, and then he was made fun of by his classmates. Therefore, in addition to learning to swim, he has a fear of swimming, a fear of the water, and remembers strongly the humiliation he suffered when he failed at swimming. Those are tougher obstacles to overcome than someone who is simply new to swimming. As a tutor when you teach segments and morsels, remember that the learner is not you, the learner is stuck, and getting him unstuck is your gift to him.

Anyone, with enough focused practice and the right teacher, can learn just about anything. Getting people who have already failed and are afraid to try again unstuck is a tremendously rewarding accomplishment. And it happens everyday in homes, schools, universities, and other settings. It is remarkable to me, and that is why I think tutors are our unsung heroes.

So, if you are like me, and you love tutoring you must have experienced the extraordinary joy of changing a life at the “one desk level”. I hope you will continue your work and I wish you much continued success.

The exemplary teacher enjoys tutoring learners one on one. She sees this as the purest form of teaching, employs a learner-centric approach, and is patient and persistent when it comes to helping the learner get unstuck.

Chapter Thirty-Three

Something to Consider

"Let your life lightly dance on the edges of time like dew on the tip of a leaf." Rabindranath Tagore

I was recently at a meeting of a school district that was working on improving teacher performance and at a breakout session I happened to ask one of the participants who were the happiest people in her organization. She quickly named three people. Later at lunch I asked another participant from the same organization the same question. Remarkably she named the same three people. Intrigued, I asked a number of people at the meeting the same question, and although the correlation was not one hundred percent, the earlier three people appeared on many of the respondent's choices.

I was probably naïve in retrospect and I had never asked this question of members of an organization before, but I decided to follow it to its logical conclusion. So I arranged to speak with each of the three people that were the consensus picks of their colleagues. One of these people was an administrator, one a teacher, and one worked in facilities engineering. I arranged to travel to the community where these individuals worked and arranged in advance to meet with each of them for approximately fifteen minutes. They all graciously welcomed my visit.

Thinking about visiting in advance I expected to meet some extremely gifted, successful, and self-confident individuals whose happiness emanated from their long list of accomplishments. After all, isn't happiness a natural result of success in life? When I met with these individuals and interviewed them I was surprised by what developed and how it was disruptive to my way of thinking.

First, as expected, all of the individuals were warm, kind-hearted, and generous. That did not surprise me. What did amaze me, however, was that they were not necessarily the most successful or accomplished employees in the organization. And, as I got to know them, I found that they were struggling with many problems in their lives. The first individual was a single mom with financial problems. By the way "facilities engineering" is another way of saying that she worked as a janitor. Another had recently had a serious health problem and her husband had lost his job. And the third, the teacher, struggled daily with a very disruptive class.

I was perplexed. So why would virtually everyone I asked list these individuals as the happiest in the organization? I asked the janitor, and like the tutor that I needed but did not know it, she answered me slowly and patiently. It was like she wanted me to get unstuck. She said:

"Happiness is not a result of things that happen in your life, although they are important, and you should strive everyday to do your best. Happiness is a choice. It is not a choice that someone makes for you. It is a choice that you make for yourself. I am happy because I choose to be happy. It is as simple as that."

Wow, that was a transformational idea for me. And as I interviewed the others they revealed essentially the same thing. Happiness is a choice that they made for themselves. Other than making that choice they had no special powers, no patent on success, and no Swiss bank account. Subsequent to that series of interviews I have queried many others about this and found essentially the same truth.

The exemplary teacher is happy essentially because she choices to be so. The old saying is "the door to happiness swings in not out", and this is information that exemplary teachers possess and share.

Chapter Thirty-Four

A Question for the Reader

"Teachers open the door, but you must enter by yourself." Chinese Proverb

I am assuming that if you have read this far, that teaching is important to you, and you are sincere about finding ways to grow and improve. Otherwise you might have stopped reading long ago. So I am delighted that you have arrived and I compliment you on your path of more outstanding work. I understand that not all of the information and ideas that have preceded this chapter are necessarily helpful to everyone. I hope you have found something helpful. As I often said to my students: lessons are like a shoe, please try this one on and see if it fits. If not come back tomorrow and we can have another lesson. I have found that few small ideas put into use can be transformative. Hopefully there have been some shoes in the preceding chapters for you to try.

The most important caveat is that the ideas must be implemented. It is not enough to say that you are intrigued, or that you like the idea, or it makes sense to you. Rather you must adopt it and implement it in you teaching. That may require changes in the way that you normally do things. It may feel awkward at first. Or, even worse it might fail. I recently interviewed an inner city high school teacher who worked diligently to get her students into college. At this particular school the dropout rate was over fifty percent, and in some years more students got pregnant or went to prison than passed their courses. But she was not discouraged. She showed me a list of thirty or so students that she was working with that she thought had the potential to attend college. I asked her how she had done in the prior year. She told me that nobody had made it into college. She was not discouraged. Actually she was quite hopeful for the coming class. Behind her desk in her classroom she had a small picture of Thomas Edison tacked to the cork-board. I asked her about it and she told me it gave her inspiration to know that it took him ten thousand tries before he got the electric bulb to light. Then she smiled broadly and reassured me that she would do better than that.

My question to you is a simple one: what are you going to do today to become a better teacher? Is there something you are thinking about trying, either in this book or elsewhere, which might make a difference for your learners? If so, let me be the first to encourage you to try. The old Chinese proverb states: "A journey of many miles begins with a single step." But before you take that first step you must take it in your mind and you must believe it might be fruitful. Actions that benefit students and potentially create improved teaching are fruitful and worth trying, even with small steps in the beginning. In that regard I wish you the best of luck.

The exemplary teacher always asks herself the question: What can I do today to be a better teacher? And when the idea comes to her she acts on it succeeding sometimes but always striving for improvement.

Chapter Thirty-Five

Is it ever too late?

"When the sun rises, I go to work. When the sun goes down, I take my rest. I dig the well from which I drink. I farm the soil which yields my food. I share creation. Kings can do no more." Chinese Proverb

Some time ago I was presenting at a conference that was helping physicians become better teachers. I am very gratified that in the medical profession most doctors feel some level of responsibility to pass on the knowledge and experience that they have obtained to the next generation of doctors. This is one of the many good things about the medical profession. As a matter of fact many university hospitals ask their physicians to volunteer to teach residents and students as a condition of their appointment to the staff. As you probably guessed the quality of the teaching that results from this arrangement is variable, not because of the volunteer's effort, but rather because most doctors, as educated as they are, have had little in the way of guidance or training as teachers. This is even more surprising when one considers that the word "doctor" is derived from the Greek word for "teacher".

After I had presented my part of the program one of the physicians spoke with me after the question and answer session. He complimented me on my ideas and thought that they generally had merit but unfortunately were not applicable to him. I asked him why and he told me that he would be retiring in a few years and it was too late for him to change what he was doing. I accepted his explanation in the haste of the moment. There were many other interesting conversations going on and I wanted to join in. Also I knew that what I had to say would not be of interest to all of the attendees. So I let his objections stand.

Later when it was quiet on the airplane I started to think about this doctor and his resistance to ideas he seemed to embrace. I thought about his excuse, that it was too late for him, and it troubled me. How could I let him get away with that? It is never too late to improve how we do things. I had read about the 102 year old who broke a swimming record, and the 100 year old who had run in the marathon, and I even knew an 81 year old who took up water skiing, so how could he, a relatively young physician say that it is too late for him to change? I decided to call him when I got home.

The next day I called him and he was quite surprised, but I think he was pleased to know that his excuses very much troubled me enough so that I would reach out to him. I told him that he was free to disagree with my ideas or come up with any other excuse that he wanted, but I would not accept his excuse that it was "too late for him to change". He found my approach slightly disarming and we have become casual friends since. I know he has changed the way that he works with his residents, and although he won't fully admit it to me I often speak to some of his colleagues who say that he has changed the way that he teaches and as a result become one of the more popular teachers.

If there is a message of this chapter it is that it is never too late for you, regardless the challenge, regardless the age. "Early" and "Late" are purely fictional when it comes to accomplishment. Those kinds of labels should never discourage a teacher from doing good things.

The powerful corollary of my example of the teacher is the student. I wish I had a dollar for every time I have heard that it is "too late" for this or that student for this or that reason. It is never too late for a student and it is almost never too late for a teacher.

The exemplary teacher never uses the excuse that it is "too late" to learn, change, or improve. These outcomes are always possible in the mind of the exemplary teacher.

Chapter Thirty-six

Helping the World to Succeed

"Remember, if you ever need a helping hand, you'll find one at the end of your arm. As you grow older you will discover that you have two hands. One for helping yourself, the other for helping others."
Audrey Hepburn

If you are the teacher of useful things you are helping the world to succeed. There is no job more powerful or important than a teacher. It doesn't matter if you teach six year olds how to kick a soccer ball or you are a tenured professor at a prestigious university. You are doing something that is simply miraculous. In a pure form you are changing a life. You are nudging achievement. You are creating mastery. With education comes a civil society. With the development of skills comes a path from poverty. With understanding comes the prospect for peace.

We live in a society where teachers are taken for granted. They may not be the most revered members of our community. They are not paid like the bankers or the brokers. But trace the skills of any star athlete, successful entertainer, leader, or businessperson and you will find a connection with one or more exemplary teachers. The teachers may have been parents, coaches, public educators, or university personnel. If they did their job well and at key times they may have made all the difference in the world. Yet they may have gone unnoticed. In a world without teachers the path of individual human experience would be drastically different.

Think for a minute about your own life and consider what it might have been like if the five best teachers that you encountered didn't take you under their wings. Maybe those mentors included a parent, a coach, or a public school teacher. I can't tell you how many times I have heard people say that they were undecided about a career path until one day they met a particular teacher. Most successful athletes can quickly credit a teacher or a coach. When I see kids in trouble or adults who struggle I always wonder if that person could have had an exemplary teacher at a critical time in his life would it have made a difference?

Despite the challenges that teachers face in today's world they still have the power to change lives. The tricky part is we don't know whose life and when, so we always have to teach at our best. And if one life is positively influenced at one teacher-learner interface our community is incrementally better off. If this forward motion is achieved in many encounters in many communities then our society is better off. And as these virtuous cycles multiply our world is better off.

In my opinion, our society should be committing much more to make certain our educational system is the best in the world. There should be an absolute commitment to making a strong public education available for every child. Resources should be deployed so that our best public teachers are attracted to schools that work with the most disadvantaged children. We live in a world where a degree beyond public school has become necessary. Yet, because of rising costs, access to college is becoming more difficult for many. If we hope to have a strong standard of living in the future we need to be constantly improving our educational system. There is no better return on investment for our society and our world than an investment in education.

And when you boil it down to the most important elements what is our educational system? Is it the buildings, classrooms, and resource centers? An important factor, perhaps. Is it the administrators, whose incomes and share of the educational dollar is growing much faster than the other components? Some might suggest otherwise. Or is it the teachers, the ones who are working with the learners everyday, adjusting their lessons to the needs of their students, dealing with the complex issues with which today's student is burdened? At its core our educational system is the teachers, and the success or failure of our system will be depend on how they do. It is a colossal burden if you think about it. But it is a call to focus on how we attract, train, support, prepare, and reward them.

We have never had a greater need for exemplary teachers in our world. When identified these "stars" need to be supported, retained, and rewarded. Additionally, we need to develop programs to grow our ordinary teachers into extraordinary ones, so that the number of exemplary teachers is always growing.

Chapter Thirty-seven

Seven Things for Today

"The beginning is the most important part of the work." Plato

If you are a teacher at any level and you are committed to improving your teaching in all dimensions there are seven things that you can begin today that will set you on a proper path. These things may seem simple but they can be transformative. First, commit to excellence in teaching. Even if you are already an outstanding teacher you know that you can make improvements. Commit today to taking the steps necessary to make those improvements. It might be helpful to reflect on your teaching with regard to the four legs of the stool. Reviewing briefly, they are your "knowledge base", your "skill set", your "communication abilities", and your "citizenship". Decide today to make improvements in all of those dimensions. Let the earlier chapters in this book be your guide.

Second, ask your learners for feedback. Ask for positive feedback and suggestions for ways that you can improve. Carefully consider this input and follow through on suggestions that are helpful. Oftentimes, learners can tell you things that you didn't realize, and sometimes their suggestions are very helpful. Commit to work on improving in areas that your learners suggest.

Third, ask your learners about their needs and concerns. As we discussed earlier the learner-centric model is one that get the learners into a fully committed participatory mode. Asking them about their needs and concerns in an open ended non-threatening way will reveal things about your learners that will surprise you. Commit in advance to addressing these needs and concerns, if possible and appropriate.

Fourth, develop at least one "case" that you can try in your unique teaching environment. Present a "case-based" session in which you are the facilitator. If problems and questions come up act as a facilitator and assign learners the task of researching the questions that arise. Follow up with them at the next session. Please give this powerful format a fair trial. It can be transformative in almost every setting.

Fifth, create a list of the healthy things that would recharge your "batteries". Commit to last least one of these activities for some definite period of time. Then evaluate if it was helpful or not. If it was continue with it regularly.

Sixth, agree to act as a mentor for another teacher or as a tutor for a student. Alternatively agree to help an educational organization that is struggling to solve a problem. Remember to employ the principles that we discussed in earlier chapters.

Seventh, thank a teacher who has helped you get to where you are. This may be a recent teacher who has influenced you or someone in the distant past. We have all had teachers who have made a difference for us. We cannot thank them enough.

The exemplary teacher enjoys completing the seven tasks assigned and commits to improving her abilities

as a teacher, her enjoyment of teaching, and her satisfaction with the results.

Additional Notes.

This book has been brought together by the thinking and collaboration of many outstanding teachers, many of whom have been my own. I would like to acknowledge all of the teachers who strive daily to make our world a better place.

The font for this edition is Hoefler Text, considered by experts to be an excellent 20th century classical typeface.

David E. McNamara, MD

Dr McNamara is available to meet with your group; as a speaker, facilitator, or participant. He is also interested in your feedback, reaction, criticism, or praise. He can be contacted at drdavidm@mac.com

www.ingramcontent.com/pod-product-compliance
Lightning Source LLC
LaVergne TN
LVHW050624100826
845148LV00011B/1720

* 9 7 8 0 9 8 2 6 9 8 2 0 4 *